Development and Rights
Negotiating Justice in Changing Societies

edited by

Christian Lund

Routledge
Taylor & Francis Group

LONDON AND NEW YORK

First published in 1999 by
FRANK CASS PUBLISHERS

Published 2013 by Routledge
2 Park Square, Milton Park, Abingdon, Oxon OX14 4RN
711 Third Avenue, New York, NY, 10017, USA

Routledge is an imprint of the Taylor & Francis Group, an informa business

British Library Cataloguing in Publication Data

Development and rights : negotiating justice in changing
    societies. – (The European journal of development research
    ; v. 10/2)
    1. Human rights – Africa 2. Human rights – Philosophy 3. Human
    rights – Africa – Case studies 4. Justice – Africa
    I. Lund, Christian
    323'.096

Library of Congress Cataloging in Publication Data

Development and rights : negotiating justice in changing societies /
    edited by Christian Lund.
    p.   cm.
    Special issue on 'Development and rights: Negotiating justice in
        changing societies' of the European journal of development research,
        vol. 10/2, December 1998.
    "In association with the European Association of Development
    Research and Training Institutes (EADI), Geneva."
    Includes bibiliographical references and index.
    1. Law and economic development. 2. Human rights. 3. Law-
    -Developing countries. 4. Legal polycentricity. 5. Cultural
    relativism. I. Lund, Christian. I.. European Association of
    Development Research and Training Institutes. III. European journal
    of development research. Vol.10 no.2, 1998 (Supplement)
    K3820.Z9D48   1999
    340'.112–dc21   98-50067
                                                                 CIP

ISBN 13: 978-0-714-64941-2 (hbk)
ISBN 13: 978-0-714-68002-6 (pbk)

This group of studies first appeared in a Special Issue on 'Development and Rights:
Negotiating Justice in Changing Societies' of *The European Journal of Development Research*
(ISSN 0957-8811) Vol.10/2 (December 1998) published by Frank Cass.

Of Related Interest

CULTURAL PERSPECTIVES ON DEVELOPMENT
edited by Vincent Tucker

ARGUING DEVELOPMENT POLICY
Frames and Discourses
edited by Raymond Apthorpe and Des Gasper

POLITICAL CONDITIONALITY
edited by Georg Sørensen

ADJUSTMENT AND SOCIAL SECTOR RESTRUCTURING
edited by Jessica Vivian

CORRUPTION AND DEVELOPMENT
edited by Mark Robinson

DEVELOPMENT AND RIGHTS
Negotiating Justice in Changing Societies

Contents

Development and Rights: Tempering Universalism and Relativism

CHRISTIAN LUND

Rights are commanding increasing attention in Development Studies but the field is mined with 'old' questions and dilemmas. This introduction discusses the question of universalism and cultural relativism. It is argued that universalists ought to recognise the relativist element in their claim and, conversely, that cultural relativists should recognise the universal element in theirs. Rather than dismissing one view and endorsing the other, we should investigate the relations between different pratices and their ideals.

'Silence!' the King called out and read out from his book, 'Rule Forty-two: All persons more than a mile high to leave the court.' Everybody looked at Alice. '*I'm* not a mile high', said Alice. 'You are', said the King. 'Nearly two miles high', added the Queen. 'Well, I sha'n't go, at any rate', said Alice: 'besides, that's not a regular rule: you invented it just now'. 'It's the oldest rule in the book', said the King. 'Then it ought to be Number One', said Alice. The King turned pale, and shut his note-book hastily.
[Lewis Carroll, *Alice in Wonderland*].

INTRODUCTION

Rights have gained interest among scholars of development societies. This probably reflects the increasing prominence of rights on political agendas in general. A great deal of research focuses on classical human rights, but other types of rights have come into focus in the context of development, some under the candidacy of human rights themselves. We talk about cultural rights, social rights, and property rights, for example, as rights to natural resources or to intellectual property.

Christian Lund, Assistant Professor, International Development Studies, Roskilde University. This collection of articles on 'Development and Rights' was first presented at the 25th Anniversary Conference of Roskilde University, Denmark, organised in 1997 by the Department for International Development Studies and Geography. The guest editor and author of this article would like to thank Signe Arnfred, Rolf Herno, Daniel Fleming, Stig Toft Madsen and Peter Friis for their collaboration.

Although variation between and within developing societies is becoming more and more incontrovertible and recognised by scholars, some elements relevant to the question of rights are probably shared by most Third World societies.

First, most legal systems in the Third World are dual, if not outright plural, whereby 'modern' legal systems and customary and religious ones develop in parallel to and in synergy with each other. This often generates ambiguity which leads to confrontation over rights and jurisdictions founded on different value systems (see Hellum, Moore and Odgard and Bentzon in this volume).

Furthermore, the political regimes of many developing societies are distinguished by authoritarian features and by the rather weak, disorganised or disparate forces of civil society. And the political forces in opposition to the state have limited capacity to turn political claims into recognised rights (see Jacobs and Kanyinga in this issue).

Finally, the development of rights in Third World societies takes place in a geo-political situation where the economic, financial, political, institutional, communicative and cultural influences of the West are significant. The influence from the rich and powerful societies on the development of rights in developing countries is multifaceted and ranges from blunt conditionalities to more subtle forms of transfer of values and ideas in benign as well as malignant forms (see Bøås in this issue). Consequently, both counter movements against Western influence on ideas about rights, and movements strongly inspired by experiences in the West relating to civil rights or minority rights amongst others have developed with increasing intensity since colonial times. The Sami-convention in the north of Scandinavia and constitutional developments in Canada and Australia are examples of this. These experiences may well have innovative potential for Third World indigenous peoples.

While rights increasingly command attention in Development Studies, the field is literally mined with 'old' questions and dilemmas. I shall discuss one of them which seems to me to be an under-current in much of the debate, namely the question of universalism and cultural relativism. The arguments of the protagonists on each side have tended to harden and become absolutist. Consequently, dialogue has sometimes degenerated into a rather sterile double-monologue of two irreconcilable claims.

UNIVERSALISM

The philosophy of universal rights is based on the idea that all humans are equally worthy of respect. Transforming this idea into policy has led to a politics of formal equalisation of rights and entitlements. As Charles Taylor [*1994: 37*] puts it: 'what is to be avoided at all costs [with this perspective] is the existence of "first class" and "second class" citizens'. The idea of universal rights is based on a conception of natural rights in which the potential of the individual human being deserves protection and the emancipation of humanity is its destiny.

Universalists argue that we need a set of fundamental moral standards in order to distinguish between 'good' and 'evil', 'true' and 'false', and 'validity' and 'power'. A number of proponents of the idea of individual natural rights argue that these principles are universal and superior to culturally embedded rights because they are neither culture-bound, nor is their genesis fixed in history (see Rorty [1984]). They are superior because we are able to deduce them from the fundamental ideas of what it is to be human.

This idea has received a number of criticisms. I shall focus on two of these. The first criticism questions how universal or transcendental these so-called universal rights are. In The Age of Rights, Norberto Bobbio [1996] shows that human rights constitute a variable category. The list of human rights has been, and continues to be, modified by changing historical circumstances. Rights, such as private ownership, which were declared absolute in the mid-eighteenth century have subsequently been subjected to radical restrictions. On the other hand, some rights which have currently acquired significance were not heard of in the seventeenth century. It is, as Bobbio [1996: 6] points out, 'difficult to see how a fundamental principle can be attributed to rights which are historically relative'. Instead, we have to come to terms with rights as socially and historically established claims which in a more or less successful process of universalisation can be variable, heterogeneous and at times contradictory.

Bobbio suggests that while rights undergo processes of universalisation, rights also proliferate in our times. Hence, it is possible to talk about rights in terms of generations, with the classical liberal rights forming the first generation and social rights, such as the right to work and the right to be free from destitution, constituting the second generation [Bobbio, 1996; Howard, 1992]. To this one might now add the right to live in an unpolluted environment, the right to personal privacy and the right to one's own genetic heritage. The development of this cluster of rights illustrates that rights develop in historical contexts, and it suggests that the creation of rights accelerates with the transformation of society. This makes political claims and their transformation into recognised rights a particularly interesting process for societies in development.

It could be argued that universal individual equal rights are indeed transcendental, if not universally respected, but have only now in modern times been conceptualised in a systematic form. This line of argument brings to mind Hegel's 'End of History', Francis Fukuyama's more recent contribution and other studies of 'The End'; a phenomenon which Upendra Baxi [1995: 1] has called 'an epistemic epidemic of endomania'. It is a line of reasoning which argues that our intellectual and moral destiny has been, or could at least be, accomplished and that all that remains to negotiate are the fiddling details.

From an intellectual point of view, this is simply not convincing. From a political point of view, it seems quite a dangerous route to follow since it precludes genuine debate over these values. Such a debate just might result in a constant acknowledgement of them as 'good'. If universal individual rights are superior, legitimising them by reference to their transcendental nature is to 'scratch where it doesn't itch'. It is not necessary; they will eventually prevail as the better argument [*Rorty, 1984: 33–4*].

This takes me to a second point of critique of universal individual equal rights, this time from a more relativist point of view. It is argued that these rights represent Western values and that recognition of them would impose Western culture. It cannot be denied that in many ways these values did originate in the West and that current Western legal and political culture is strongly influenced by them. And it cannot be denied that Western culture, in a broad sense, has often been promoted in the name of universal individual equal rights. Moreover, this 'export of culture' has often violated one of its own self-justifying principles, that is, cultural sensitivity and tolerance. However, criticising certain values as Western imposition tends to conflate Western political philosophy with liberalism and to ignore other Western philosophies, such as communism, social democracy, conservatism and fascism, which hold different values [*Howard, 1993: 222*]. A critique of certain values and of Western imposition of culture is warranted in many cases but it must be substantiated and contextualised.

CULTURAL RELATIVISM

I shall now move on the argument of cultural relativism and a critique thereof. This form of relativism accords primacy to culture. Cultural relativism assumes that there is no culture whose values and customs dominate in a moral sense. This means that every culture has an equal right to be different, distinct and unique. And it is often argued, at least implicitly, that culture is the supreme ethical value and that culture-bound values are superior to extra-cultural values [*Howard, 1993: 319*]. This idea has also received criticism of various kinds and here I shall focus on two points.

The first point questions how culture-bound the idea of cultural relativism is itself. The claim that one ought to act in accordance with the principles of one's own culture and that all cultures should enjoy equal respect, is a universal moral principle *par excellence*. Thus, cultural relativists do not fully reject universal ethics as they claim to do. Furthermore, in many societies this claim would be considered extra-cultural, and thus it cannot even be seen as universally valid. The question is whether the cultural relativist claim is not as universalising in scope as the claim for universalism itself.

Further, the fact that the very notion of rights constitutes a genuine Copernican revolution, that is, a change in how we view the world, should not be ignored. Emphasis is no longer on people's and groups' duties toward the state and wider society, but on individuals' and groups' rights *vis-à-vis* the state and wider society [*Bobbio, 1996: 39*].

A second kind of critique has been directed against cultural relativism. Cultural relativism is often presented in a form which essentialises cultures [*Eriksen, 1997; Hansen, 1997*]. Crudely, the argument runs somewhat like this: 'Our culture constitutes a homogeneous whole with a certain balance of indigenous values; and exogenous values cannot be transferred to such a society.' In some cases this line of argument is little more than a sorry romanticist veneer serving to cover the diversity within a specific culture and to suppress those groups who subscribe to different values. And what about the 'cultural bastards' who straddle two cultures and who are 'no longer' culturally pure? It is worth remembering that social movements for political change arise precisely because we *do* envisage and claim rights or entitlements which we *do not* presently enjoy. And through social and political struggles such claims are sometimes turned into recognised rights and hence, a part of culture, I suppose.

OPPOSING ABSOLUTISM

In sum, where does all this leave us? At a general level, what I call for is that universalists recognise the relativist element in their claim and conversely that cultural relativists recognise the universal element in theirs. This could be a first step towards what Charles Taylor [*1991: 72*] terms a 'work of retrieval'. Instead of dismissing one view and endorsing the other, maybe we ought to investigate the relation between different practices and their ideals. In other words, we ought to identify and articulate the higher ideal behind more or less debased practices in order to make more palpable what the different principles we might subscribe to really involve. This would also enable us to criticise acts and policies that justify themselves rhetorically by reference to values without there being any substantive link between them [*An-Na'im, 1997*].

It also entails engaging in a work of persuasion. This is, of course neither possible nor desirable if you assume an absolutist standpoint but it is the appropriate policy according to the view I am advocating here. To be a bit polemic, one could say that while the point of departure for this 'work of retrieval' involves an ethically neutral approach to the substantive questions of liberal universalism and cultural relativism, we must adopt a rather absolutist approach to the procedures by which we engage in this work both as academics and citizens: that is, an investigation of rights in terms of their moral content as well as the processes of application in practice and in transformation in search of 'the better argument' in dialogue. One could argue that this belief in Reason reflects a romantic belief in the merits of the Enlightenment and is bound to be unsuccessful given the inherent defects of Enlightenment thinking. However, my contention is that the defects of the Enlightenment can only be made good by further enlightenment and that the totalised critique of reason undercuts the capacity of reason to be critical [*Habermas, 1996; McCarthy, 1995: xvii*]. The following two contributions by Zygmunt Bauman and Per Bauhn continue the discussion of universalism and relativism in theoretical terms. They both reject absolutism but do so from two quite different positions.

REFERENCES

An-Na'im, Abdullahi A., 1997, 'The Contingent Universality of Human Rights: The Case of Freedom of Expression in African and Islamic Contexts', *Emory International Law Review*, Vol.11, No.4. pp.29–66.

Baxi, Upendra, 1995, 'The Unreason of Globalization and the Reason of Human Rights', mimeo.

Bobbio, Norberto, 1996, *The Age of Rights*, Oxford: Polity Press.

Eriksen, Thomas Hylland, 1997, 'Multiculturalism, Individualism, and Human Rights: Romanticism, the Enlightenment and lessons from Mauritius', in R.A. Wilson (ed.), *Human Rights, Culture and Context*, London: Pluto Press.

Hansen, Thomas, 1997, 'Inside the Romanticist Episteme', *Thesis Eleven*, No.48, pp.21–41.

Habermas, Jürgen, 1996, *Between Facts and Norms - Contribution to a Discourse Theory of Law and Democracy*, Cambridge: Polity Press.

Howard, Rhoda E., 1992, 'Communitarianism and Liberalism in the Debates on Human Rights in Africa', *Journal of Contemporary African Studies*, Vol.1, No.1, pp.1–21.

Howard, Rhoda E., 1993, 'Cultural Absolutism and the Nostalgia for Community', *Human Rights Quarterly*, No.15, pp.315–38.

McCarthy, Thomas, 1995, 'Introduction', in J. Habermas, *The Philosophical Discourse of Modernity*, Cambridge, MA: MIT Press, pp.vii–xvii.

Rorty, Richard, 1984, 'Habermas and Lyotard on Postmodernity', *Praxis International*, Vol.4, No.1, pp.32–44.

Taylor, Charles, 1991, *The Ethics of Authenticity*, Cambridge, MA: Harvard University Press.

Taylor, Charles, 1994, 'The Politics of Recognition', in C. Taylor *et al.*, *Multiculturalism*, Princeton, NJ: Princeton University Press, pp.107–48.

On Universal Morality and the Morality of Universalism

ZYGMUNT BAUMAN

Plurality is the condition sine qua non *of freedom. And there is no morality without freedom. Adherents of a universalist strategy argue that good people have no use for freedom; that freedom is clamoured for by those bent on making wrong choices. Yet is is unbecoming of adherents of a pluralist strategy to believe the contrary – that freedom is a sufficient guarantee that goodwill be chosen over evil, and that once we take care of freedom, goodness and beauty will take care of themselves. Further, it is wrong to assume that what is chosen does not matter providing it has been chosen freely. Freedom is there to prod responsibility and assist in making good choices.*

In a recent programmatic paper 'Against Moral Relativism', Rom Harré [*undated*] pointed out that 'the postmodern insight, that at any moment an indefinitely large cluster of stories could be told about the human situation then unfolding' is 'disturbing to moral philosophers'; they, moral philosophers, and Harré among them, believe that 'to recover a serious morality arguments must be constructed in defence of some form of moral absolutism'. Harré is not the first and most probably not the last philosopher to declare anxiety in the face of plurality of opinions, and to express the conviction that only elimination of that plurality, or disqualification of all opinions but one, may allow a 'serious morality', that is the proper separation of good from evil.

In voicing such declarations, moral philosophers expressed more than their own professional beliefs. They gave a learned form to the embarrassment of the ordinary men and women bewildered and confused by the need to choose and to bear consequences of that choice – as well as to the strategies of the legislating powers determined to spare them that agony. The sole professional peculiarity of the philosophers' responses to the polyvocality of moral voices is their conviction that getting rid of the agony it causes depends on the 'arguments to be constructed', and that it is the philosophers who are called and predestined to construct them.

That a human being can be human in more than one way and that it is not immediately evident to all which of those ways is preferable, is an offputting,

Zygmunt Bauman, Professor, Department of Sociology, University of Leeds, UK.

upsetting and distressing thought. Not because there is something intrinsically odious and repulsive about plurality itself, but because of the vexation it is likely to cause the acting person. The primordial, baseline discomfiture and irritation is that of the uncertainty how to act; plurality breeds a lot of such uncertainty since it means that different people follow different rules and so it is not easy to guess which rule will be applied in response to one's action. Imagine yourself having to take part in a game in which other players follow rules of their own choice and in which there is no telling what those rules are at the moment or are likely to be next – and you will get the inkling of the subliminal anxiety that plurality of the ways of life is able, if not bound, to provoke. For this reason the possibility that many stories may be told about the human situation and that there is no evident way of reducing them to just one story is, indeed, disturbing.

The paradox, though, is that there can be no escape from the agony of choice except through a choice – a choice of strategy; and that none of the strategies one can choose boasts the kind of 'absolute grounding' which will have made the choice between them not truly a choice. The road to non-arbitrary rules leads through an arbitrary decision … .

As long as plurality remains the fact of life, there are conceivably but two principal types of strategies which one can choose from when hoping to mitigate its distressing impact. The boldest, the most thorough and radical, and for that reason the one most obvious to choose, is the strategy to do away with plurality itself, a strategy that aims to replace diversity with sameness and thus to do away either with plurality itself or with its relevance and its 'nuisance power'. The other strategy does not promise quick and radical solutions and therefore it is often denigrated as the sign of capitulation or denounced for not being a strategy at all. In its weaker version, the second strategy assumes that plurality is here to stay; and that, therefore, in order to make human cohabitation possible one needs ground rules for negotiating the moot points and agreeing to disagree while avoiding the dire consequences of disagreement. In its stronger version, the second strategy makes the virtue out of necessity, declares plurality to be good and sets to make the best of it in order to make human cohabitation better.

It is the acceptance of the first strategy which obliges the chooser to invoke the idea of *universalism* – but we can go a step further and say that 'universalism' is that strategy by a different name. Whenever one postulates *universally binding* rules of conduct in general, moral rules in particular, what one says are two things: first, that liking certain rules, being familiar with them or feeling at home in a world cut to their measure are not sufficient reasons to follow them; and that among many competing rules there are some which have other, stronger reasons to support them than erratic human passions or accidents of history, and so stronger claims on human obedience. The trick is to pass by, ignore or incapacitate the contingencies of passions and history and to go straight to those 'stronger reasons' from which the universal rules may be deduced.

The two assumptions tacitly present in the invocation of 'stronger reasons' are not just an oblique way to define the universal rules; they amount as well to an exercise in division. They divide the realm of rules into the rules worth their name and non-rules or pseudo-rules or 'mere opinions' masquerading as rules. They *assert* as they *disqualify*. The implicit objective of the exercise is to replace the dialogue with a monologue, by denying other participants of the dialogue the rights of the speaking subjects or invalidating in advance the relevance of whatever they may speak about. Like in the ideal objective of Habermas's 'undistorted communication' – the essence of something being 'last' and 'ultimate', the status which universal rules, being universal, have the sole right to claim, is the invalidation of the very possibility of questioning it; and so the cancellation of that uncertainty which made the search desirable, but also possible, in the first place.

Where exactly the 'stronger reasons' may be found is itself a contentious matter, and many suggestions have been made in the long history of philosophical quarrels. But as always in similar cases, the major contention is between *discovery* and *invention;* between *finding out* what are the rules which ought to be universally followed though for some reasons are as yet – time and again, here or there – ignored; and *designing* the rules which because of their own power of persuasion, or some other powers which render ignoring them unlikely, are bound to be universally followed once spelled out. To put it in a different form: the essential quarrel is between the idea that the observed human freedom of choice is a sham or a regrettable deviation from the straight and preordained path, while in fact the universally applicable rules are ready and waiting to be read out and obeyed – and the idea that although human freedom is real and genuine, it needs to be used to choose self-limitation by replacing variety with sameness and so indirectly to deprive itself of its object and work itself out of the job. The first of the two ideas competing in the promotion of universalism of rules is that of *universality*, the second that of *universalisation.*

This has been a shorthand account of the adversary ideas that underlie the positions taken in the debate, not of the tactics the sides use in the actual combat. In those tactics the above-mentioned division all-too-often proves unworkable and is not easy to maintain. As Roland Barthes pointed out many years ago, the substance of all myths is to represent *history* (that is, something human-made and so something that can be un-made or remade by humans) as *nature* (that is, something not of human making and thus something which no human effort may change, let alone undo). The myth of universal rules is no exception. And so on the one hand the protagonists of universality, who announce the discovery of pre-human, supra-human or otherwise stronger than human rules, still face the fact that their audience must be convinced that discovery is valid; their discoveries need first to be accepted as universal before they become universally binding and so something must be done to bring about this acceptance and make it stay. In other words, the idea of universality will be ineffective – indeed toothless – unless complemented by the tactics of universalisation. On the other hand, however, even the outspoken promoters of *positive* law, that is, of the law explicitly man-made and authoritatively enforced, find themselves obliged to locate the reason for limiting human freedom outside that freedom – and so to present their invention as, in the last resort, a discovery.

This having been said, there is still an important difference between the views deriving human sameness from an underlying unity that precedes all social or individual choices (from 'divine order', 'natural law' or 'human essence'), and the views which ground the hope in that sameness in precisely those choices – the laws and the ideas which will eventually make essentially alike all people who are at present, due to the diversity of legislative ideals and habits, fundamentally different. The latter view, we may say, is more akin to the modern spirit, which is marked by the ordering zeal and sees the human condition as a problem rather than a limit imposed in advance upon the legislative freedom; as a task which needs yet to be fulfilled with the help of human wit and resources.

This second view, indeed, prevailed in modern philosophical reflection – much as it pervaded modern political practice. Even when 'natural law' was invoked as the ultimate authority, it was always up to the 'rational law' to make it operative. Something was always yet to be done to replace discord about values and norms with consensus – and that 'something' boiled down in the last account to the institution of the right kind of laws and obtaining obedience to their letter and spirit. Universality was in modern practice the *end product,* an achievement of universalisation, even when in theory it was taken to be and presented as its starting point, justification and the guarantee of its ultimate success.

Nature or reason, 'natural' or 'rational' law – the quandary haunting all varieties of universalism is always the question of how to select out of the multitude of contradictory ways of life the one and only which is destined one day to become universal. From Montaigne on, all philosophers *could* be aware and many *were* indeed aware that powers-that-be tend to represent the rules and norms which they happen to prefer as dictated by nature or reason, and so universal in their essence and offering the best choice there is for every human being; and that therefore the rules promoted as universal may under closer scrutiny prove to be symptoms of parochialism in disguise. But to be aware of the danger is not the same as to escape it; as a matter of fact, most efforts were directed at stifling the suspicion, arguing it away, declaring it null and void. The more habitualised are the ways and means of one's own land the more they feel to 'stand to reason', to be the 'natural way' of doing things, particularly if seen against strange and alien ways and means, which feel odd or mistaken. But, as Cornelius Castoriadis put it succinctly and pithily in his 'Radical Imagination and the Social Instituting Imaginary':

> ... when one moves, as the last Husserl and the first Heidegger, from the egological, strictly phenomenological point of view ... to the 'life-world', one has just exchanged the egocentric for an ethno- or sociocentric point of view: solipsism on a larger scale. For, to know, as we must, that our *Lebenswelt* is but one among the indefinite number of others is to recognise that there is a multiplicity of 'first person' 'collective experiences' among which there is, at first glance, no privileged one; at second glance, the only 'privileged' one philosophically and, I would add, politically – is the one which made itself capable of *recognizing* and *accepting* this very multiplicity of human worlds, thereby breaking as far as possible the closure of its own world [*Castoriadis, 1997: 325*].

Few philosophers, if any, did in actual fact avoid the trap set by the insidious tendency of socially instituted habits to disguise or reincarnate as reason – even if they explicitly and earnestly warned against the assumption that reason resides only in one's own country and kept repeating that what is different from one's own idea of truth is not necessarily wrong just for being different. As Tzvetan Todorov showed in his study of nationalism, racism and exoticism in French thought, most of the models for universal morality launched by the philosophers of moral universalism were but home truths raised to the status of universality; many of the models were straightforward tautologies (as, for instance, Pascal's argument about universality deserved by Christianity: since no other religion taught us that men were born in sin, no other religion but Christianity spoke the truth) [*Todorov, 1989*]. Despaired of the pervasive and pernicious threat of parochialism, Husserl spent his life developing a method to purify the truth-searching reason from all contamination with history, culture, emotion – in short, with 'mere existence'. To confer on reason unconditional superiority over history, culture, emotion and proclaim its independence from all those lesser beings was a bold, yet nevertheless arbitrary choice – and a very modern, very European one, to be sure.

Given the breath-taking inventiveness of the human mind, it is remarkable that only one method of putting such doubts to rest by representing the choice as not a choice but necessity has been found and practised in the modern era. Johannes Fabian [*1983*] gave that method the name of *chronopolitics*. It consisted in casting the lateral, contemporaneous diversity upon the timescale, and so representing the different as obsolete, a relic of the past that outlived its time and now exists on a borrowed one, carrying a no-appeal death verdict carved all over its body. To do so took but few relatively simple mental operations.

First, the idea of universalisation as a gradual process of making the different alike was projected on the flow of historical time; what was born in the modern world as an intention pressed against the future was stretched back to the beginnings of mankind. Once that has been accomplished, the rest was easy: hidden behind the twin shields of historical progress and imperialist project, the contents of the 'universal model' were secure from questioning, secure even from the need to justify themselves argumentatively. It was *obvious* that speeding up the wheels of progress, lifting the backward and spreading the good news of the proper form of human existence was the 'white man's burden'. The contents of the 'universal model' were nothing else than the values and norms that happened to be values and norms of the carriers of that burden.

The stratagem of chronopolitics depended from the start on the support of two closely related authorities: that of the idea of history as a process of gradual, but relentless *universalisation*, and the practice of extending the Western, modern rule with the view of making it sooner or later truly universal. The persuasive power of chronopolitical assertions could last as long as the authority of those two authorities remained unquestionable. This, though, is no more the case.

The strength of the twin authorities has been eroded simultaneously from the top and from the bottom. The grip in which the West held the rest of the world and which was expected to tighten as 'the time marches on' is softening, and rapidly. Still half a century ago any part of the globe not under the administration of one or another European country or its overseas settlements was seen as 'no man's land', sooner or later to be assigned to the Western jurisdiction. Today even the tiniest spot of the globe can successfully claim sovereignty and more often than not is gladly granted it – sometimes even despite its residents' wishes. Its sovereignty may be a sham as far as military and economic self-sufficiency go, but it most certainly covers the right to decide locally which of the values and norms on global offer are right and proper for the local residents.

The idea of objective superiority of certain values and norms which used to justify the claims to universality made on their behalf does not arouse much excitement among the powers-that-be in the West, whose hopes for global rule are now grounded in financial and trade ascendancy which may only gain from political and cultural dispersion and diversity. Neither does it impress the former dependencies of the West. Such Western inventions as tanks, mines and machine-guns, private cars, burglar alarms and fast-food joints, occasionally also anti-epidemic vaccines, may be readily embraced while refraining from treating Western Civilization as a package deal; to get the cars and the tanks, one does not need to engage in the philosophical debate about universality of Western values, abandon the native styles, nor abstain from digging up from oblivion, or inventing, one's own cultural tradition.

To cut a long story short: the times of 'assimilation', when 'lower' cultures were prompted and sooner or later eager to efface their difference in the name of the values and styles of the 'higher culture', are by and large over. From whatever side you look at it, *difference is today an asset* rather than a liability and those different from the dominant majority may reasonably expect to gain rather than lose from guarding and displaying their idiosyncrasies.

No wonder that nowadays one does not hear much of 'universalisation'. Instead, one hears quite a lot of 'globalisation' – a concept quite unheard of at the time when 'universalisation' loomed large in daily discourse. This conceptual change of guard is symptomatic – one can say that the change of the message is itself a message. If 'universalisation' stood for courage and determination, 'globalisation' stands for resignation and lack of resolve. Universalisation was what one does or intends to do; globalisation stands for what is happening to us in an internet-like messy world into which all seem to be putting their fingers but of which no one is, or can truly be, in charge. Universalisation was to be the work of the all-powerful law of history aided and abetted by the unified code of reason; globalisation emerges from the contingent interplay of uncoordinated and mostly anonymous forces. Finally, universalisation was to result in the 'sameness' of human beings; globalisation, on the contrary generates new cultural diversification as it smothers and levels up or down the extant differences in economy and material trappings of daily life.

The point, however, which seems to me more crucial than any other, is that the idea of universalisation needed to be and has been elbowed out by that of globalisation because there are simply no forces left self-confident and resourceful enough to undertake what the *project* of universalisation entailed. Such forces which truly dominate the world today thrive on exploiting the differences, not the similarities – and show no interest nor display any zeal in promoting actively the unification of mankind and all its works. But – let me repeat – the discourse of universality tends to remain inconsequential unless supported by the determined universalising effort. Without universalising powers, universality is no more than a construct of the philosophical debate which, as Wittgenstein sadly observed, 'leaves everything as it is'. Universality may be the universalism's gospel, but universalising action is its sword. And so I put it to you that if universalism has fallen presently on a bad patch, it is not because of the drawbacks of the universality discourse, lack of ingenuity in putting together a convincing argument, or other failings of ethical philosophers – but because of the waning of that universalist, proselytising and converting spirit alive throughout the modern era, together with the modern social arrangements and modern global balances of power which fed it and gave it the air of a realistic objective.

Where does all this leave the question of moral discourse? If two centuries of flirting with 'moral absolutism' fell flat without an issue, is a 'serious moral discourse' still possible? To an orthodox ethical philosopher the answer is an emphatic 'no', and that 'no' is a good reason to be worried.

This worry is not the result of an empirical observation that nowadays, when 'moral absolutism' falls into disrepute or reveals its impotence, more people than before and on more occasions confuse good with evil and more evil deeds are committed. Whether this is indeed the case, is after all highly debatable. The nostalgically-recalled by ethical philosophers 'high modernity' times, when the search for the one and only universal and ultimate rational ethical code went on unabated, were not known after all for their heightened sense of morality and a panic retreat of evil. Most atrocious crimes in the history of humanity have been committed in the name and for the sake of the absolute truth and ultimate good. Concern with the ultimate, irrevocable verdict of Nature and Reason did not stop crimes from being perpetrated; if anything, it helped to commit them and justify them once committed, because the 'finality' of all final truth, 'universality' of all universal justice means precisely the *permission to disregard all truths but one* and to consider proper all injustices that are believed to bring the universal justice closer. As the age-old folk wisdom has it, the perfect is the enemy of the good – while whoever looks for absolute perfection makes many enemies.

Besides, shifting the problem of moral choice to that of obedience to the rule, and so to conformity to the will of the stronger rather than to responsibility for the fate of the weaker – that trade-mark of the universalist strategy in its orthodox edition – leaves the objects of ethical regulation incapable and unwilling to make moral judgments of their own and shoulder responsibility for their consequences. This may not be a big problem in the running of daily business and in everyday routine, but it tends to swell to catastrophic proportions once the trained conformity is deployed by evil powers for evil purposes.

Consider the following parable. Mother is taking her child for a walk. A stray dog runs by and the child wants to stroke it. Mother tells the child not to do so, and the child, expectedly, asks why. There are three ways in which mother can answer that question. She may say: 'Because I say so'. Or: 'stray dogs are dirty, you may get ill'. Or: 'You may frighten the dog; dogs have reasons to be afraid of children, because some children are cruel and like to inflict pain'.

From the point of view of instrumental reason, all three answers are of equal value, providing they achieve their purpose, which is to stop the child from stroking the dog. From the moral point of view, they are however miles apart. The difference comes from the fact that while the *instrumental value* of response is measured solely by obedience to whatever it demands, the *moral value* of the answer may only be measured by the increase or decrease of moral capacity in the person to whom it is addressed. And the moral capacity consists in the capacity and the will *to take the point of view of the other and the good of the other as seen in that view for one's prime concern* even if no rule commands one to do so in a given case; and to *take responsibility for one's responsibility* for the other's good – also for one's responsibility for the other's right to define that good.

When judged by moral standards, the first two answers are at best amoral, but they may be immoral in their consequences. The first answer is at least sincere and unashamedly calls for obedience; more exactly, for taking the will of someone stronger, of someone able to reward and punish (in this case the mother), for the principle of one's own behaviour. Do what you are told, as long as the person who is telling you to do so has the power to coerce you into submission.

The second answer makes allowances for the child's thinking ability, appeals to the child's reason by suggesting that the command should be followed because it is good for the child; an expedient regularly used, as Michel Foucault pointed out, by all 'pastoral' powers, which present their rule as service to the ruled – deemed to be incapable to understand, unless told, what is good for them and so unable to attend to their own well-being on their own, but able to see what is in their best interest when properly directed to it. The second answer also defines obliquely the meaning of that 'good' which ought to justify obedience to the rule: that 'good' is the actor's own benefit, the actor's pleasure or avoidance of pain. What you do to others is good or bad depending on the effects it will have on your own condition. The principle is the same as in the first answer: follow the rule because if you don't you will be punished. The sole difference consists in the charging of the stray dogs, rather than the command-giver herself, with the capacity to inflict pain. Mother should be thanked for the warning; stray dogs must be avoided or chased away.

Only the third answer appeals to the care for the other. It does not promise rewards nor threaten punishment. It does not justify the need of care by the power of the other to get what the other wants. On the contrary, it points out that it is the other who will suffer from the actor's disobedience, not the actor himself. The actor is strong, he may take action or desist from taking it without penalty in any case. It is the other who is weak and helpless to stop the harm which the action may bring.

The third answer, therefore, appeals not to the actor's responsibility *to* (this or that power), but to his responsibility *for* (someone powerless). The dog is powerless precisely because it does not give commands, does not spell out what the child should do, and anyway has no means to force the child to do what it, the dog, wants. That 'taking responsibility' which the third answer implies does not mean that the child should be (as it would when following the other two answers), an executor of somebody else's will, only this time of a different kind of 'somebody'. After all, the child may only suspect and does not know for sure what the dog indeed wants; it is this uncertainty which demands that the child visualises the dog's wishes, and there is no knowing for sure that the visualisation will be correct.

To conclude, the *peculiarity* of the third answer lies in its appeal to the actor's *freedom*. It points out that the actor is free to choose, that the choice is his and his alone – and that this is precisely why whatever choice the actor makes in the end he will have but himself to blame for. The third answer does not offer anything that in the logic of instrumental reason would pass as a rational argument against the pleasure of stroking the dog. There is no hint of a power able to coerce child to be guided by the dog's welfare. There is no hint either that to care for that welfare, to avoid inflicting pain, 'stands to reason', promotes the child's interests or makes good business sense. It says: 'you do not know and you won't know what to do; all the greater, therefore, is your responsibility for what you are doing – so think carefully about the effect your action may have on others'.

I have dwelt on that 'dog stroking' parable rather longer than the brief and rather trivial event of meeting a dog in the street would demand, but there was good reason to do so. The story offers an insight into the reasons why morally concerned persons should not necessarily bewail the failure of the 'universalist' strategy and why they ought not necessarily be appalled by the growing evidence that plurality and polyvocality, rather than being temporary irritants, tend to remain permanent features of the human condition.

As Jean-Jacques Rousseau already pointed out more than two centuries ago, solely the choice made by a free person refers the action to the actor's responsibility and therefore allows it to be judged as good or bad. The choice (a not-pre-determined choice and one that is made in the situation of unclarity) is the birth-place of a moral person and the homeground of morality. Not only that much feared uncertainty does not preclude 'serious morality', but on the contrary, it is precisely the situation of not-knowing-for-sure-what-to-do that makes moral responsibility serious; it prods, wakes up, calls out the moral self in the acting person and lowers the chance that moral considerations will be dismissed as irrelevant to his or her action. The question of the action being 'good' or 'bad' is confronted in all its seriousness when that action is *not* a 'command-following' step, when it is not clear which authority is entitled to command – and so the actors cannot assign responsibility to anyone but themselves.

ON UNIVERSAL MORALITY AND THE MORALITY OF UNIVERSALISM   17

And so we have come to the second of the two strategies mentioned at the beginning. You may take the preceding considerations as a defence plea on behalf of the 'stronger version' of that second strategy which, as you remember, starts from the assumption that 'plurality is good for morality' and proceeds 'to make the best of the chance it creates'. Plurality is the condition *sine qua non* of human freedom. And there is no morality without freedom. Humans come across the problem of setting apart good from evil because they have to choose between more than one possibility to act, and they come to grips with that problem in the practice of choice.

The partisans of the universalist strategy suspect deep in their hearts – often despite their outspoken beliefs and the opinions they would be ready openly to endorse – that good people who know well how to proceed have no use for freedom; that freedom is clamoured by those bent on making wrong choices, and that once obtained freedom is likely to be used solely for evil. Yet it is unbecoming of the pursuers of the other, the pluralist, strategy to believe the contrary – that freedom is a sufficient guarantee that goodwill be chosen over evil, that (as Richard Rorty says) once we take care of freedom, goodness and beauty will take care of themselves. And it would be downright wrongheaded for them to assume that once freedom has been achieved there is nothing left to be done, and that what is chosen does not really matter providing that whatever is chosen has been chosen freely. *What is chosen does matter a lot;* it is the only thing that does matter in the end. Freedom is there to prod moral responsibility and thus to help make good choices. A free human being is one who has no excuse for not making them.

Good choice starts from the willingness to care for the Other, which is the expression of respect for the Other's *dignity*. But the care for the Other risks being wrong-footed unless it is linked from the start with tolerance – which is the sign of respect for the Other's *freedom*.

One universalist precept irremovably present in the pluralist strategy is the postulate of universality of human rights, understood as the right to be and remain different. But this kind of universalism does not boil down to the resigned acceptance that humans will probably stay different and that nothing can nor should be done to make them more alike; if this was the case, the recognition of human rights would amount to sheer indifference, to washing one's hand of all responsibility for the fate of others. The universal right to difference has no moral value unless it is a product of freedom; that is, unless humans are truly free in both the negative and the positive sense of freedom, and so they have the resources enabling them to choose what they genuinely wish to choose and to sustain their choices.

Choosing the form of humanity for others is an exercise in power, not morality. But declaring neutrality regarding that form, whether it was willingly chosen or surrendered to for the lack of choice, is a symptom of callousness, not the moral stance. It is *caring that the others have what is necessary to make their choices freely which lies at the very heart of morality.*

Plurality is the starting point and the end point of moral engagement with the Other. Thanks to plurality, partners may confront each other as moral subjects and so enter a dialogue in which their common presence in the world they share can be negotiated without putting the rights of any one of them in jeopardy. But contrary to Jürgen Habermas, the purpose, the horizon of that negotiation is not a consensus which would put an end to that plurality which prompted the moral engagement in the first place, but making the plurality of human ways more secure and so preserving and reproducing the conditions of the dialogue, the conditions of morality.

Yet (and this is why Habermas's protestations against 'distorted communication' must be carefully heeded) moral engagement would be barren, were it confined to dialogue without making sure that the participants of the dialogue are indeed free to choose the form of life which sets them apart from the others. In the present world we are far from having made sure that freedom is the property of all; and the deepening polarisation of access to the means needed to exercise freedom of choice and of the rights to mobility shows that we are not coming closer to that situation. In the world which has no other resource to rely on in its struggle to improve on its own morality except the moral responsibility of free agents, the active promotion of the universality of free self-assertion is the crucial and the most urgent of moral precepts.

REFERENCES

Castoriadis, Cornelius, 1997, 'Radical Imagination and the Social Instituting Imaginary', in C. Castoriadis, *The Castoriadis Reader* (edited by D.A. Curtis), London: Blackwell.
Fabian, Johannes, 1983, *Time and the Other: How Anthropology Makes Its Object*, New York: Columbia University Press.
Harré, Rom, n.d., 'Against Moral Relativism', mimeo.
Todorov, Tzvetan, 1989, *Nous et les autres: La réflexion française sur la diversité humaine*, Paris: Seuil.

Universal Rights and the Historical Context

PER BAUHN

A common assumption of communitarians and other moral relativists is that the idea of universal human rights cannot apply to societies outside the modern Western world. Their argument is that since a valid morality cannot but reflect the values that are actually held in this or that society, and since universal human rights are not generally recognised in pre-modern and non-Western societies, there are in fact no universal human rights. In this essay the communitarian argument is criticised on the grounds that it does not distinguish between positive morality (that is, what people, as a matter of fact, believe to be right and good) and normative morality (that is, what people should *believe to be right and good, were they fully rational). Moreover, it is argued that a normative understanding of the morality of universal human rights need not involve us in any anachronistic reasoning about the moral character of people in ancient or culturally distant societies. Nor does it imply a rejection of what is sound in a communitarian argument about the importance of historical contexts.*

The term 'universal rights' refers to rights had by all humans, in all times, and in all cultures. As will be clarified below, 'had' should be understood in a normative way. In this essay I intend to discuss three criticisms of universal rights theories concerning the alleged inability of such theories to account for the importance of historical context. The criticisms are as follows:

(1) that universal rights can have no valid application outside the rather modern and Western historical context in which they were formulated;

(2) that evaluation of institutions and practices of the past should not be based on universal rights, but should reflect the historical context of these institutions and practices;

(3) that universal rights for their effectuation in a political community presuppose that the members of that community share a common identity, provided by a particular historical context.

Per Bauhn, Senior Research Fellow, Department of Sociology, Lund University, Box 114, S-221 00 Lund, Sweden.

In what follows I will argue that (1) and (2) can be rejected, and that (3) does not constitute a serious problem for a theory of universal rights, but can be accounted for within the frameworks of such a theory. As I proceed I will also present the outlines of a rationally justified theory of universal rights to freedom and well-being.

The view that rights can only exist within a historical context which actually recognises them (the first objection above) is a point often raised against defenders of theories of universal rights, the implication being that since not all kinds of human societies have recognised human rights such theories must be mistaken: rights are in fact not universal.

Ancient Greeks and Romans were, for instance, slave-holders and slavery was legal in their societies. Feudal lords and vassals, to be sure, engaged in extensive debates over their respective rights, but it never occurred to them that *all* human beings were equally entitled to the same rights. Writing about the values of feudal knights historian Carl Stephenson notes that:

> Gallant gentlemen, it would appear, had no antipathy to violence and cruelty; within the accepted rules of combat they were expected to be bloodthirsty and ruthless. And whatever courtesy they displayed was reserved for members of their own order. For a knight to live by war and rapine, pillaging churches and slaughtering peasants on the lands of an enemy, was quite normal. Women he properly regarded as at most a valuable commodity [*Stephenson, 1942: 53*].

In fact, this criticism continues, human rights appear on the political agenda first in the contexts of the American Declaration of Independence and the French Revolution, both events of the late eighteenth century, and it is another century before such an important right as that of voting in political elections is acquired by a significant part of the population in the Western world. Such fairly modern contexts excepted, there is no general recognition of human rights, and hence theories of universal rights are simply wrong. To talk of rights without their being embodied in a social order and legally recognised is simply pointless. 'Lacking any such social form, the making of a claim to a right would be like presenting a check for payment in a social order that lacked the institution of money' [*MacIntyre, 1985: 67*]. Now, this line of argument need not really trouble a defender of universal rights, at least not as long as the conception of rights held is normative and not positive. Rights in the positive sense are those rights that are actually recognised in a particular community, while rights in the normative sense are the rights people *should* recognise, that is, that are justified whether people actually believe so or not. (This distinction is modelled upon one between positive and normative moralities, formulated by Alan Gewirth [*1994: 22-3*].)

It can be plausibly argued that the very existence of many conflicting positive moralities, as when Ayatollah Khomeini pronounced that Salman Rushdie morally deserved to be killed as a blasphemer and Western countries denounced the Ayatollah's sentence as morally wrong, points to the need for a normative conception of morality and rights.

> For the conflicts raise the normative question, which goes back at least to the Hebrew Bible and to Socrates: Which of these positive moralities, if any, is valid or justified, as against its various rivals? This question adduces a normative concept that is distinct from the positive concept, for it asks not, What is recognized, believed, or accepted? but rather, What is morally right or valid, so that it *ought* to be believed and accepted? [*Gewirth, 1994: 26*].

Accordingly, the fact that rights have not been universally recognised will not count as an objection to a *normative* theory of universal rights, since such a theory does not dispute this fact, but rather claims that there are rights that *should* have been universally recognised. Still, such a normative position may be held to be unreasonable, since it seems to be too indifferent to the conceptions of right and wrong that have actually guided people in different historical times. Michael Walzer, for instance, argues that

> Justice and equality can conceivably be worked out as philosophical artifacts, but a just or an egalitarian society cannot be. If such a society isn't already here – hidden, as it were, in our concepts and categories – we will never know it concretely or realize it in fact … Men and women do indeed have rights beyond life and liberty, but these do not follow from our common humanity; they follow from shared conceptions of social goods; they are local and particular in character [*Walzer, 1983: xiv–xv*].

How Walzer's account of rights works is shown in his discussion of education as a part of distributive justice. Whether publicly funded education should be offered to all children is, he argues, a question of how welfare rights are perceived in the particular community in question:

> Welfare rights are fixed only when a community adopts some program of mutual provision. There are strong arguments to be made that, under given historical conditions, such-and-such a program should be adopted. But these are not arguments about individual rights; they are arguments about the character of a particular political community. No one's rights were violated because the Athenians did not allocate public funds for the education of children. Perhaps they believed, and perhaps they were right, that the public life of the city was education enough [*Walzer, 1983: 78–9*].

It should be noted that Walzer's argument addresses the importance of a shared conception of rights in order for these rights to receive legal or other official recognition within a particular community, rather than the question of the justification of rights. And as long as his discussion is confined to what is causally necessary for rights to be implemented, the normative universal rights theorist need not have any quarrel with him. The question of what rights are morally justified is different from the question of what it takes to have rights socially accepted and enforced, which Walzer also seems to recognise as he observes that the Athenians *perhaps* were right in their view of the right to education.

Walzer's argument, however, points to another objection against theories of universal rights, namely, that it would be unfair to criticise the Athenians because they did not apply a universal conception of rights, for instance, by accepting slavery. This constitutes the second historicist criticism of universal rights listed above: that evaluations of past institutions and practices should reflect the historical context of these institutions and practices. The unfairness consists in charging ancient communities with violations of rights which they could not possibly have had any conception of, given the concepts and meanings that they actually shared.

A similar criticism is implied by Bernard Williams in his defence of a 'relativism of distance', according to which we should refrain from passing moral judgements on societies that are at a certain distance from ours, whether in time or in space:

> Of some traditional societies, isolated and non-literate, it may have been straightforwardly true that they did not know that there were alternatives, but many sophisticated hierarchical societies, those of the European Middle Ages for instance, certainly knew of alternatives, inasmuch as they knew that human beings had organized societies in other ways and did so at that time elsewhere. What they did not know, we shall have to say, is that there was an alternative *for them*. But then it is far from clear that there was an alternative for them. We need some firmer hold than we presently have on *what might have been* to say (at any interesting level, at least) that they might have had a different social organization, and some even more robust view about freedom to say that they could have attained it [*Williams, 1985: 164–5*; original emphasis].

Now, the accusation of being unfair need not bother the universalist too much. What he claims is that the institutions of ancient societies which did not respect universal rights were morally wrong, but this does not necessarily imply that the people operating these institutions and believing them to be justified were morally blameworthy. When it comes to administer praise and blame it certainly matters if the people under consideration could have thought or done otherwise.

Here we should judge mistakes in moral judgements as we do judge mistakes in empirical judgements. We now know that the earth rotates around the sun and hence that the heliocentric, not the geocentric, view of the universe is the correct one. But we also know that this view was not available to our ancient ancestors, at least not to a majority of them. Accordingly, we do not blame them for their ignorance, since it is not intellectual laziness but rather lack of access to relevant knowledge that deprived them of correct beliefs. Hence, it is not *necessarily* the case that morally wrong institutions and practices automatically make the agents of these institutions and practices morally blameworthy. It all depends on whether these agents could have believed otherwise or not.

In some of the most obvious cases of violations of rights, such as the torturing to death of heretics or rebels, it could be plausibly argued that the agents of this torture should not have needed any sophisticated modern theory of rights in order for them to know that what they were doing would at least be *prima facie* morally wrong. After all, killing and inflicting harm on human beings have been condemned in all known moral traditions and have always been thought of as needing very rigorous justification if ever undertaken.

But perhaps many of those who engaged in such violations of basic rights in ancient communities actually believed that they were justified in doing so, and not just acting from hatred, greed, envy or other less respectable motives. (We should bear in mind that those who today defend the death penalty do not necessarily advocate their position out of personal vindictiveness.) And maybe these persons of ancient communities were prevented by powerful institutions (such as the church in medieval times) from questioning the reasons that were supposed to justify their deeds. Then we may well find room for exculpating them from moral blame, while still holding that their moral beliefs were wrong.

On the other hand, we may find it harder to exempt the people in charge of powerful institutions who tried, often successfully, to prevent a free discussion of alternatives to the prevailing conceptions of the right and the good. At least these persons may be said to have known of such alternatives, since the very efforts they made to prevent people from adopting new ways of thinking and evaluating indicate that they really thought of these new ways as alternatives which *could* be realised if they were not subjected to severe repression.

We should also be aware that the fact that there seems to have been very little criticism of, for instance, slavery in ancient Athens, does not mean that such criticism could not have been formulated by ancient Athenians. As Michele Moody-Adams has pointed out, since even the poorest Athenian benefited from the institution of slavery, at least in the sense that it made it possible for him to view himself as a member of an elite of free-born persons, there would be a strong temptation to ignore all anti-slavery arguments:

All these considerations suggest that the support of ancient Greeks for the institution of slavery could well have embodied their choice to perpetuate an institution that benefited non-slaves in various ways. The belief that slavery was justified was insufficiently examined by those who held it. But there is no convincing evidence that the blame for this should be traced to anything other than the affected ignorance, in Aquinas's phrase, of those who wanted to perpetuate the culture of slavery. Affected ignorance – choosing not to know what one can and should know – is a complex phenomenon, but sometimes it simply involves refusing to consider whether some practice in which one participates might be wrong [*Moody-Adams, 1994: 296*].

Now, one reason why universal rights theories have been accused of being ahistorical and socially disembodied may have to do with the intuitionistic and ad hoc character of the premises of some of these theories, which seems to reflect little more than the attitudes of this or that philosopher. Robert Nozick [*1974: ix*], for instance, asserts rather than argues that 'individuals have rights, and there are things no person or group may do to them (without violating their rights)'. A similar intuition is expressed by Ronald Dworkin in his description of rights:

Individual rights are political trumps held by individuals. Individuals have rights when, for some reason, a collective goal is not a sufficient justification for denying them what they wish, as individuals, to have or to do, or not a sufficient justification for imposing some loss or injury upon them [*Dworkin, 1978: xi*].

However, there are more to universal rights than mere intuitions. A cogent justification of moral rights in terms of the logically necessary claims of rational agents to possess the generic goods of agency has been developed and defended by Alan Gewirth.

Gewirth's theory is as simple as it is brilliant. Human agency, being central to all moral prescriptions (regarding what we should or should not *do)* constitutes a reasonable point of departure for a normative moral theory. Hence, Gewirth begins by analysing the features that necessarily pertain to all actions, that is, the *generic* features of action, which he defines as *voluntariness* and *purposiveness.* In order for any human behaviour to be called an action it must be freely undertaken by the agent (voluntariness) and guided by her intention to achieve a particular goal (purposiveness) [*Gewirth, 1978: 27*].

Now, all action is evaluational, due to its inherent purposiveness: the agent acts because she *wants* to achieve a certain goal, and by her very action she subscribes to the evaluation that this goal constitutes a good for her, at least in the minimal sense of being something that she prefers to see realised rather than not realised [*Gewirth, 1978: 39–41*]. (This does not imply that the achievement of her goal will *do* her good: her goal may be to smoke 20 cigarettes within an hour, or take a swim among the piranhas.)

Different agents can be expected to have different conceptions of what goals are worth trying to achieve and hence to be considered as goods. But all agents must (logically) regard the conditions generally necessary for successful agency as *necessary goods,* since without them no agent can hope to realise her particular goods, that is, her particular goals of action.

Given the generic features of action (voluntariness and purposiveness) the generally necessary conditions of successful action will be *freedom* and *well-being.* Together they constitute the *generic goods* of agency, and the rights that rational agents will claim to them will be the *generic rights.* Freedom includes that the agent controls her action by her own informed choice. Well-being has three dimensions. *Basic* well-being involves being alive and healthy, enjoying physical integrity and mental equilibrium. *Non-subtractive* well-being is about maintaining one's level of purpose-fulfilment, that is, not having one's capabilities for action diminished. It hence designates primarily negative conditions, such as not being subjected to robbery, defamation, and harmful conditions of housing and work. *Additive* well-being is about increasing one's level of purpose-fulfilment, that is, improving one's capabilities for action. It designates primarily positive conditions, such as education, employment, income and wealth. It also includes various dispositions of character such as courage, temperance, and prudence [*Gewirth, 1978: 52–8, 211–13, 232–7, 240–45, 249–55*].

Now, Gewirth argues, all rational agents must (logically) claim rights to freedom and well-being. How is such a move, from needs of agency to rights-claims regarding the objects of these needs, possible? What is essential here is the *normative structure* of action. Evaluation is intrinsic to action, since all agents, as we saw above, view their particular goals as goods, and their freedom and well-being, as being the generally necessary conditions of successful agency as necessary goods. The fact that freedom and well-being are *necessary* goods means that the agent cannot accept that other agents interfere with her possession of them, that is, she claims rights to them. To accept such an interference would be equivalent to accepting that her goals were not goods at all to her, and that she did not care as to whether she achieved them or not. But by engaging in action she has already committed herself to viewing her goals as goods. Hence, not to claim rights to freedom and well-being would involve the agent in a self-contradiction:

> Suppose some agent were to deny or refuse to accept the judgement (1) 'I have rights to freedom and well-being.' Because of the equivalence

between the generic rights and strict 'oughts', this denial of (1) would entail the agent's denial of (2) 'All other persons ought at least to refrain from interfering with my freedom and well-being.' By denying (2), the agent would have to accept (3) 'It is not the case that all other persons ought at least to refrain from interfering with my freedom and well-being.' But how can any agent accept (3) and also accept (4) 'My freedom and well-being are necessary goods?' That he must accept (4) we saw above; for by virtue of regarding his purposes as good the agent must also a fortiori value his freedom and well-being as required for achieving any of his purposes [*Gewirth, 1978: 80*].

And since a rational agent recognises that it is in her capacity *as an agent,* or at least as a prospective agent, that she must claim rights to freedom and well-being, she must also accept that all other agents are entitled to the same rights-claim [*Gewirth, 1978: 109–12*]. Hence, all rational agents must from the normative judgement 'I have, *qua* agent, rights to freedom and well-being' infer the normative conclusion '*All* agents have rights to freedom and well-being', embodied in the *Principle of Generic Consistency* (PGC). 'Act in accord with the generic rights of your recipients as well as of yourself' [*Gewirth, 1978: 135*].

Hence, the PGC prescribes for all agents an equality of rights to freedom and well-being. It should be noted that this equality of rights also includes economic democracy and redistributive taxation whereby vast inequalities in power between owners of capital and the poor, or between capitalists and employees, are mitigated. (The realisation of economic rights is the major subject of Gewirth's recent book *The Community of Rights* [*1996*].)

Having said this much about the derivation of the PGC from the conditions of successful agency, I will go on to the implications of this principle for political communities and historical contexts. The protection of the equal rights of all agents justifies instrumentally the existence of a state, which in its minimal form maintains basic rights by criminal laws and in its welfare form protects supportive rights to additive goods such as education and employment and thereby helps its citizens to develop and exercise their abilities as agents [*Gewirth, 1978: 290–304, 312–19*].

The state as justified by the PGC constitutes a *community of rights,* since it is not only the case that the state contributes to its citizens having effective rights to freedom and well-being, but by virtue of this contribution the citizens have and accept obligations to their society. This is what Gewirth calls the *social contribution thesis,* describing the supportive mutuality characterising the relationship between a just society and its individual members:

The community of rights, then, means not only that the community supports the rights of its members but also that those rights support the community insofar as its support of its members' rights both enables and obligates them to support the community. The members' contribution to the society as a community of rights may range from the work they do in providing exchange values whence they derive income, through paying taxes to support the community, to much more heroic contributions in military service and other ways of protecting the society. But in all such modes of action the relation of mutuality is paramount whereby persons fulfill one another's needs and rights. They have obligations to the society as enabling the development of this mutuality [*Gewirth, 1996: 84*].

This view of the community of rights raises the question of the importance of historical context, as it is formulated in the third objection to universal rights theories above, namely, that the community of rights presupposes a previously existing political community which has provided its members with a collective identity, based on features such as a common language and a shared history. That is, the mutuality essential to the community of rights cannot be accounted for simply by pointing to the state's protection of rights in that community. If there was not already a historical community with a strong sense of collective identity and solidarity, the community of rights would not be feasible. Hence, rights are at least for their effectuation in the constitution of a particular political community dependant on a historical context providing the members of that community with a common identity. In the words of Will Kymlicka:

The sort of solidarity essential for a welfare state requires that citizens have a strong sense of common identity and common membership, so that they will make sacrifices for each other, and this common identity is assumed to require (or at least be facilitated by) a common language and history [*Kymlicka, 1995: 77*].

According to Kymlicka, a community of rights or any other political or moral project would not constitute a meaningful option in the absence of a historical-linguistic context that provides it with a meaning:

Whether or not a course of action has any significance for us depends on whether, and how, our language renders vivid to us the point of that activity. And the way in which language renders vivid these activities is shaped by our history, our 'traditions and conventions'. Understanding these cultural narratives is a precondition of making intelligent judgements about how to lead our lives [*Kymlicka, 1995: 83*].

Gewirth, however, does not deny the importance to the individual of her being historically situated. On the contrary, he explicitly acknowledges the merits of the communitarian doctrine of the self as being at least partly constituted by its communal roles:

It brings out that the sense of belonging, of being part of a larger nurturing whole, is a valuable component of human additive well-being. It serves to emphasize that what exist are not bare, abstract individuals such as figure in many traditional theories of natural rights, but rather persons whose self-identity and self-awareness are partly constituted by their being members of specific cultural groupings demarcated in terms of family, race, class, gender, nationality, ethnicity, religion, ideology, neighbourhood, occupation, and other partly interpenetrating variables. The doctrine also brings out the historical locatedness of human selves, for the communities to which they belong and in which they function have definite historical dimensions [*Gewirth, 1996: 91*].

Gewirth's conception of the community of rights is, however, about the normative mutuality of rights and obligations that should characterise the relationship between individual citizens, and between the citizens and their state. It is not a tale of the origins of political community of the kind provided by earlier political philosophers such as, for instance, Rousseau. Hence, there is no necessary conflict between Gewirth's (normative) view of the just society and Kymlicka's (empirical) idea of the causal importance of language and history for the forming of a communal identity.

Nevertheless, this does not seem to be quite a satisfying response to Kymlicka's argument. If it is true that without community there would be no community of rights, and that without common language and shared history there would be no community, should not language and history be counted among the necessary goods of the community of rights (analogous to the way in which freedom and well-being are considered to be necessary goods for all agents, due to their importance for all agents' particular goals)? And should not the preservation of their language and history be an obligation for all citizens of a particular community? And would this not entail that we are, in the end, forced to move from universal rights to the ethnocentric state, and that historical context finally has got the upper hand in the competition with moral universalism?

Now, it is important that we are careful about exactly what Kymlicka's argument can and cannot establish. At its best it seems to have a good case for concluding that language is essential to the identity of *cultural* communities, since one reason why people may perceive themselves as members of a common culture is that they share the same language. But from this it does not follow that *political* communities, that is, states, necessarily must be defined in terms of a common language, since one political community may include more than one cultural community. And as a matter of historical fact, membership of a certain linguistically defined community does not always determine a person's political affiliation, as when German-speaking Alsatians preferred to remain French rather than be members of Imperial Germany, to which they were annexed by force in 1871 [*Zeldin, 1980: 77–83*].

That a political community need not be monolingual is shown by the example of Switzerland, where German, French, and Italian are official languages of the state. Likewise, the republic of Finland includes a minority of Swedish-speaking people whose language enjoys an officially recognised position beside Finnish. And the political community of Spain includes Catalans and Basques, and so on.

Of course, a political community cannot avoid making decisions about what language(s) should be recognised as the official language(s) of the community in question. The democratic procedure, justified by the PGC as protective of and expressing the right to freedom, requires

> a system of civil liberties whereby each person is able, if he chooses, to discuss, criticize, and vote for or against the government and to work actively with other persons in groups of various sizes to further his political objectives, including the redress of his socially based grievances [*Gewirth, 1978: 308–9*].

The exercise of these civic liberties obviously presupposes that the policies of the government and the arguments for and against them are available to all citizens in a language which they all understand. Hence, having some language(s) made official or national is *instrumentally* necessary to the workings of the democratic procedure and hence justified by the PGC. (This instrumentalist justification should not be confused with the ethnicist and essentialist argument that the nation-state should preserve the national language because it is the carrier of the national identity or essence.) A language's being made official means that it is taught to all children as their first language, and that it can be used by all citizens in their dealings with the public institutions of their political community, including hospitals, libraries, police, and so on. The adoption of an official language is a good in itself, since it entitles all citizens to expect that the language they have learned in school will be the one used in their everyday encounters with public institutions as well as in the laws and politics of their community.

Sometimes more than one language is given official status, at least within some region of the political community that is bilingual, or where one of the community's minority languages is in fact the dominant language. Whether a political community should be monolingual or bilingual is, however, more a question of pragmatic politics than of moral rights. Bi-lingualism may, for instance, be a way to promote a minority culture's identification with the larger political community and so increase overall national solidarity, which would be a good thing for all citizens. This, however, does not entail that mono-lingualism in a multicultural political community would necessarily constitute a violation of moral rights. (And we should bear in mind, that even communities which recognise two or three official languages may still have cultural minorities whose languages are *not* recognised as official.)

The members of a minority culture do not have their rights to freedom and well-being violated just because their children are educated in a language which is not that of their parents. In fact, a beneficial aspect of a monolingual education policy may be that it enables the younger members of a minority culture to communicate with their fellow citizens of the wider community, and thereby to participate in the political process of that community. Hence, monolingualism may well enhance political equality. However, the government *does* violate the rights of the members of a minority culture if it, for instance, prevents them from giving their children additional education in their own language, or interferes with their freedom to communicate with each other in speech or writing (including in the form of books and newspapers) in that language.

After this rather extensive discussion of the necessity of a common language to the community of rights, we should turn to Kymlicka's argument that a common history is necessary to the communal identity. Here we must distinguish between the importance of a shared *history* and the importance of a shared *conception* of history. Kymlicka's argument is, I believe, about the latter, since he refers to our 'traditions and conventions', which seems to imply shared *beliefs* about a common past, rather than just a shared past. Now, we may entertain more or less mythical beliefs about the glorious or humble origins of our nation (as, for instance, the Romans' myth of Romulus and Remus), which it is the professional duty of historians to scrutinise against known facts. But these various conceptions of history are more likely to be the *outcomes* rather than the preconditions of communal identities, reflecting an already existing community's way of perceiving itself.

However, I do believe that a *shared history,* in the sense of a factual background of a common socio-political order, is essential to the understanding of communal identities in general, and hence also to the understanding of the preconditions of the community of rights. I will suggest, as an empirical hypothesis, that the background conditions that explain the collective identity necessary to the mutuality of the community of rights are to be found in the socio-political order that defined its predecessor community. This predecessor community, which I will call the *community of obligations,* was characterised by sharply defined inequalities and clear divisions into, on the one hand, privileged classes as those of the nobility and the clergy, and, on the other, mere subjects, among whom we will find peasants and day-labourers. Furthermore, it was characterised by the rule of the few over the many, and obedience rather than freedom, emphasising obligations rather than rights (hence, the name of the community). The existence of such a community of obligations is exemplified in the histories of all pre-modern Western political communities, as well as in the ancient political communities of the Orient, such as China and Japan.

Those who by the institutions of the community of obligations were defined as mere subjects, and not included within the privileged orders, thereby received a common identity which, once (and if) they were given the opportunity to see through the justifications of the existing order, they used as a mobilising force against the ruling classes. This occurred, for instance, when the third estate constituted itself as the French *National* Assembly in 1789, or when the working classes of Europe late in the nineteenth century began to organise themselves in unions and political parties under the banners of socialism to bring democracy, civic rights, and welfare reforms to their societies.

So, the community of rights depends indeed for its existence (but not for its justification) on an earlier community of obligations, the struggle against which causes subjects to constitute themselves as a nation of citizens, and so assume control over the continuous project of their political community. In this way, the normative universality of rights can be shown to be consistent with the particularity of a historical context, as a nation of citizens creates new political institutions designed to protect the universal rights within the territory of their political community, without this particularity detracting anything from the (normative) universality of the rights in question.

Consequently, the community of rights need not be ahistorical and disconnected from the evolution of actually existing political communities. But nor need it depend for its moral justification on the historically given, as some communitarians would want to have it. The conception of the community of rights as a rationally justified model of society for its members to strive for within a continuous, ongoing particular political project hence brings together normative thinking with an empirically ascertainable historical context.

REFERENCES

Dworkin, Ronald, 1978, *Taking Rights Seriously*, Cambridge, MA: Harvard University Press.
Gewirth, Alan, 1978, *Reason and Morality*, Chicago, IL: University of Chicago Press.
Gewirth, Alan, 1994, 'Is Cultural Pluralism Relevant to Moral Knowledge?', *Social Philosophy and Policy*, Vol.11, No.1, pp.22–43.
Gewirth, Alan, 1996, *The Community of Rights*, Chicago, IL: University of Chicago Press.
Kymlicka, Will, 1995, *Multicultural Citizenship*, Oxford: Clarendon Press.
MacIntyre, Alasdair, 1985, *After Virtue*, London: Duckworth.
Moody-Adams, Michele, 1994, 'Culture, Responsibility, and Affected Ignorance', *Ethics*, Vol.104, No.2, pp.291–309.
Nozick, Robert, 1974, *Anarchy, State, and Utopia*, Oxford: Blackwell.
Stephenson, Carl, 1942, *Mediæval Feudalism*, Ithaca, NY: Cornell University Press.

Walzer, Michael, 1983, *Spheres of Justice*, Oxford: Blackwell.
Williams, Bernard, 1985, *Ethics and the Limits of Philosophy*, London: Fontana Press.
Zeldin, Theodore, 1980, *France 1848–1945: Intellect and Pride*, Oxford: Oxford University Press.

Changing African Land Tenure:
Reflections on the Incapacities of the State

SALLY FALK MOORE

State legislation and international development agencies may envision grand programmes revising African systems of land tenure, but local pressures and competitive struggles actually determine many of the terms and conditions of African land holding. This contribution shows how such programmes can be frustrated by the strategies of individuals. It shows that actions on the small scale can cumulatively demolish state policy without the individuals involved ever being collectively mobilised in movements of resistance. Though claims to land in Africa can be translated into human rights terms, this analysis proposes that if human rights discourse omits the political and practical aspects of implementation, it is not very useful.

Property in land is surely one of the most socially embedded of the elements of a legal order. It is a truism that property is not about things but about relationships between and among persons with regard to things [*Hohfeld, 1919; Ellickson, 1991*]. In short, to say that someone has a right to land is to summarise in one word a complex and highly conditional state of affairs which depends on the social, political and economic context. The place, the setting the history, and the moment, all matter.

The title of this study, 'Changing African Land Tenure' has a double reference. Not only are local pressures and struggles continuously changing the terms and conditions of African land tenure, but vigorous efforts to control and direct land entitlements by national authorities and international agencies have also been around for a long time. Periodically a radical reshaping of African land tenure regimes is predicted or advocated. This is the case at present. Current crises are invoked to justify the urgency of such proposals. Depending upon the political commitments of the speakers, the allusion to trouble focuses on different, negative aspects of the current situation and matching solutions. Commonly alluded to are the deteriorating state of the physical environment, the demographic explosion, the absence of political democracy, the presence of corruption, the need for economic development, the danger of intergroup

Sally Falk Moore, Professor, Department of Anthropology, Harvard University, William James Hall, 33 Kirkland Street, Cambridge, Massachusetts 012138, USA.

violence and other serious troubles and inequities. Among the many strategies advocated for a better future, legal changes are often urged, affecting constitutional/political matters, property regimes and human rights. The implied assumption of the talk about legal change is that laws can both be easily put into place and easily implemented. This paper is a small sceptical commentary on that proposition (see also Low [*1996*] and Scott [*1998*].

Having limited space, I will illustrate with a few instances how certain recent programmes to create equitable redistributions of property have been frustrated. The method used here is one that uses events as its initial data. The implications embedded in a small diagnostic event are traced outward to infer larger social processes [*Moore, 1977; 1986; 1987; 1993*]. First, I will describe a single case history from East Africa, the instance of a well-to-do woman whose present land-holding situation embodies not only the immediate exigencies of a post-colonial world, but is demonstrably connected with at least a century and a half of changing property relations, including the Tanzanian experiment with socialism.

In the second part of this study I want to reflect on current talk about proposed land policies for West Africa. The search for general solutions to West African problems, legal solutions among others, leads to flights of the utopian imagination. Because the states of the region have nationalised land, serious people go so far as to project the possibility of a total redefinition of property interests in the course of de-nationalisation and governance reform. One might have supposed that no such grand change by legislative means would be thought possible, given the variety and importance of local property practices in West Africa, and the limited effectiveness of the states involved. What interests me here is a particular aspect of this problem: the way, under various conditions, little people can dismember state policy. Local persons with personal and local concerns often can undo grand plans of reform. The instances I have in mind are not organised movements of collective political resistance. Seemingly trivial actions of individuals can demolish state policy just as effectively.

AN ILLUSTRATION FROM EAST AFRICA

In 1993, Sophia confided to me that she had much to worry about. She was engaged in a complex negotiation over a house she had once owned in one of the principal towns of Tanzania, and things were not going well. She acquired that piece of real estate in an unusual manner. In the last decade of the colonial period, she was the mistress of a British officer and had borne him a son. When the Brits left, the officer, who had a wife and son in England, left with them. However, he was an honourable fellow and wanted to take care of the woman and son he had left behind. At some time before independence, judging correctly that no Chagga patrilineage would give any of its patrimonial lands on Kilimanjaro to the son of an Englishman, he bought Sophia a substantial house and land in a town about fifty miles away from Kilimanjaro. In the colonial period, urban land was outside of the customary law system and was transferrable as freehold [*James, 1971: 100*]. But in rural areas, 'native law and custom' governed [*ibid.: 62–3*]. Sophia did not live in the town house, but rented it out to some foreign entrepreneurs. Her residence was on rural Kilimanjaro in her widowed mother's very comfortable dwelling. It stood in the midst of a small farm-garden with a banana grove, coffee trees, a cow or two.

When Independence came in 1961, Sophia intended to keep her urban property for her young son and planned to transfer it to him when he came of age. She knew that neither she nor her son would ever inherit her mother's house. It was patrimonial land owned by Sophia's father in his lifetime. When he died his widow, according to Chagga custom, was entitled to continue to live there. But when the widow died, it normally would revert to a male member of the patrilineage chosen by them to succeed.

However, when Sophia's mother died the men of the chiefly lineage did not reappropriate her land, though it was their legal right to do so under 'customary law'. They let Sophia stay on. Why did they modify the norms of patrilineality in this way? There were two reasons; one was that Sophia had, by that time, already lost the town house, and they wanted to take care of her. But there was a more instrumental reason than solicitude for her well-being. All of the men of the patriline already had plots of land that they occupied on Kilimanjaro. They were afraid that if any of them took another parcel, local members of the ruling party would denounce them and confiscate the property. Government decrees about landholding were interpreted by the party as meaning that one could legitimately occupy only one plot of land. 'Surplus' property would be confiscated.

What was the reasoning behind the Tanzanian 'one piece of property' policy? When Tanzania became independent of British colonial rule in 1961, there were a few things which President Nyerere thought absolutely inimical to the egalitarian, socialist ideal which he had in mind for the nation. One was the kind of officialised inequality represented by the existence of chiefs. Therefore chiefship was abolished. The other was the 'parasitical' exploitation of tenants implied by the very existence of landlords, who were by definition extracting income without working for it. Every possible measure was to be taken to disempower such an undeserving elite. For Nyerere, landlord–tenancy arrangements were clearly one of the more wicked aspects both of feudalism and capitalism.

To ensure that landlordism would not continue, all titles to land were appropriated by the state in 1963.[1] All that citizens could 'own' was the right of occupancy, or beneficial use. And under the new land law, land that one was not occupying and using could not be kept. Thus, it became apparent that Sophia would have to sell the town house that was to have been her son's inheritance. She was especially vulnerable because chiefly families like hers were the targets of particularly vengeful party practice. And, of course, some desirable properties confiscated for 'the people' found their way into the hands of Party officials or their relatives.

Sophia solved the two-property landlordism problem as best she could. There was a foreign company doing business in the city where her townhouse was located. For some years she had rented the house to the company for the use of one of its executives. Once the single property rule came in, she changed her arrangements with the company. They would buy the house, so that nominally it was theirs, and the local party ideologues who were confiscating second properties would not then be able to take it away from her. The secret oral condition that accompanied this transfer was that when and if the socialists ever lost power and there were no longer any strictures against multiple tenures, she would be able to buy back the house. The company agreed, but the matter was not put in writing as it was plainly illegal.

Since 1985, the liberalising pressures from the World Bank have committed Tanzania to a return to privatisation, and eased many of the restrictions that the socialists had placed on property-holding. Sophia wanted the town house back. Her son was reaching adulthood and she had to worry about his future.

The company did not deny that it had made the agreement to re-sell the house to her and were willing to do so. The obstacle was the *price*. Sophia insisted that under the original agreement they were to let her buy it back at the price at which she had sold it to them. But that had been more than 25 years earlier. Inflation in Tanzania has been horrendous. The company wanted a more realistic price, some approximation of market value. Sophia did not have the necessary money. In a letter to me about a year ago, she said the matter had still not been settled.

The details of Sophia's situation were unique, but her transfer of property to surrogates to conceal continued ownership was not. Scattered all over Kilimanjaro there were relatively well-off individuals (though by no means all as affluent and elite as she) who deposited second properties with nominal surrogates during the more orthodox period of socialist party practice. All of them are now free to try to get them back. This is happening outside the courts, outside of any formal legal system. Since the arrangements were illegal and made because of the government threat of confiscation, there is no tribunal to whom these people can appeal. The state had not deprived them of the property directly, so no rights argument about restitution of property taken without compensation would have been available even if there had been some hearing agency at hand.

What is visible about property law and national policy in this abbreviated case history? Side by side, and, interdigitated in the life experience of Kilimanjaro residents are a plurality of simultaneous legal, illegal, and non-legal orders, rules and practices that originated in different historical periods. Individual transactions come in and out of public view, involving different aspects of this complex. The ideologies in play at various times have ranged from all that surrounds the patrilineal bond, to the socialist logic of an inspired leader, to the development rationale of the World Bank. Drawing on different pieces of this experience people try to combine strategies of self interest with strategies of self-respect. National development policy and the public welcoming of capitalist strategies by all and sundry, (today, even by Nyerere himself) legitimises current self-seeking. But it went on even when the official ideology preached sharing, egalitarianism and brotherhood. Sophia lost on the townhouse deal, but she may succeed with a more recent experiment in landlording, the expansion of her mother's house to accommodate paying guests.

For Sophia and all the others, the law, and the breaking of it or the keeping of it is only one element of many in the management of a life. Myriad such local settings transform the meaning of property and the significance of national legal interventions all over Africa. They are not mobilisations of collective political action, but they can undo the plans of a government as effectively as if they had been.

However, taking such actions into account on a national policy level is a difficult thing to do, especially when it is not clear what is happening or how often. As Herbert Simon [1957: 199] wrote long ago about 'the principle of bounded rationality', decisions are rational in relation to the simplified model we construct of a situation, not necessarily in relation to the real world itself.

RECONFIGURING LAND LAW TO RECONFIGURE A SOCIETY

What I want to do now is to move from the details of the small scale local event to the large scale international palaver. I shall comment on the themes that have appeared in policy-oriented discussions of West African land and which I have heard as a consultant in recent years and have seen in related publications of the OECD, USAID, CILSS and others. Prominently absent from most proposals for the future are allusions to the predictable illegalities and distortions of direction that are likely to occur. The only one that often elicits comment is the abuse of official authority by agents of the state [Thomson and Coulibaly, 1994]. New versions of this critique of the central state have recently reappeared in connection with the policy of government decentralisation sponsored by the international donors. The focus on repairing past problems by changing the form of the postcolonial state seems to have distracted attention from other issues. The way the informal strategies of local people may redirect the implementation of policy have not had sufficient authoritative attention.

Writing in a regional synthesis, commissioned for one of the international meetings on this topic, Gerti Hesseling and Boubacar Ba have no hesitation about saying:

> Thirty years of reform, amendment, adaptation and patching up of the law in the different Sahelian countries have produced some laws of undoubted quality; some are gems of legal technique, others contain original solutions. Nonetheless, since 1980 it has been recognized everywhere that Sahelian land legislation is not readily enforceable at the local level. Almost everywhere land legislation (in the broadest sense) is seen as an obstacle to fair, balanced, environmentally conscious development [*Hesseling and Ba, 1994: 30*].

Environmental conservation and economic development loom large in the discourse about land law reform. But other issues figure as prominently. Also addressed are: security of tenure, democratic management, equitable access to land and other resources, and conflict resolution. Each of these terms is a label for a host of implied political meanings. As World Bank conditionalities have shifted so have the significances of these labels.

International policies directed toward a free market economy, privatisation, democracy and decentralisation of political control, will have major implications for rural land tenure. But what those implications are remains in debate. As political attention shifts from an exclusive preoccupation with the capitals of West Africa to the countryside, and as more and more Africans are drawn into the discussion, there is increasing acknowledgement of the diversity and importance of local social configurations. Land tenure reform is no longer being approached from an entirely unitary, state-centred logic, founded in most of these countries on a history of land nationalisation. But the problem of balance between state and local control has not been worked out [*Mamdani, 1996*].

Policy discussions relating to land law in the Sahel are all skewed by the existence of state nationalisation. Thus 'security of tenure' for the 'peasants' may be read in part as a euphemism for the uncertainties associated with de-nationalisation. For the moment, most states in the Sahel do not seem ready to do much about de-nationalising. The state has the 'domaine' in the Francophone countries and the 'title' in the Anglophone. Sufficient paper gestures have been made in the direction of privatisation to keep the flow of international money coming. Thus, for example, not without some urging from the World Bank, a law was passed in Burkina Faso in 1991 to the effect that land in the national Domaine 'may be assigned as private property' [*Faure, 1995*]. Nevertheless, the principle that in Burkina the state still holds the national 'domaine' continues to prevail, and the possibility of private landholding remains a reality only on the books.

One example of changing intellectual conceptions of the situation is described in the work of Professor Etienne Le Roy. At the University of Paris, he has long led a research group on land tenure questions (APREFA).[2] Summarising the shifting attitudes that surrounded its work in recent decades, he says that in the 1970s the theorisation of APREFA was Marxist in concept. At that time, he tells us, the basic distinction made was between 'traditional' and 'modern' systems. Those categories had an evolutionary thrust. The assumption was that private property was the future.

Dissatisfied with that stance in the 1980s, APREFA adopted a different nomenclature, and characterised African land tenure systems as being in a state of 'transition'. But by 1996 Le Roy says he even finds the theme of 'transition' problematic, since it seems to continue to signify an evolutionary direction. He now prefers to say that land in Africa is a form of patrimony that figures in an economy of redistribution. He sets up a series of definitions, labels and models that he contends follow from such an analysis. This then prepares the way for his critique of a 1995 World Bank document which prescribes private property as the necessary solution to present problems in African land tenure [*Le Roy, 1996: 335*].

Le Roy is undoubtedly describing accurately the sequence of intellectual attitudes in a particular circle in France, and there are many there and elsewhere who have their doubts about the panacea of individual ownership. But his own generalised redefinition of the esprit of African property in land does not clarify matters. He is proposing a unitary definition of the underlying essence of African land tenure. But is there need for such an essentialist reduction?

To me, any such essentialist analytic path is quite a distance from the multiple, shifting, permutating, recombining practices of rural Africa. As Etienne Le Roy is very much aware, there is a huge diversity of local 'systems', and Africans operate simultaneously in multiple legal milieux, as even the outline of Sophia's story indicates. The question is how to address such a complex, and how to understand the way it has been addressed in recent decades by insiders and outsiders.

The outsider view is easier to capture than the multiple insider ones. As I see it the major recent shifts in the international donor discourse relating to land tenure are closely linked to the major political changes that have taken place from the 1980s on. During the cold war, for political reasons, rural economic development was treated as an encapsulated entity, as a technical problem. It was approached as if it had no political dimensions. At that time, rural *governance* was not a topic in the mouths of Western donors. Rural change was conceived in terms of local projects to increase production, and thereby to alleviate poverty.[3] The emphasis was on agronomy and technology. State policies regarding the administration of the countryside were not to be questioned. States supported by the Western international community in the interest of the Cold War were not to be criticised openly. The social organisation of the countryside as a political issue was untouchable. The alleviation of poverty was the acceptable rhetoric.

Now the whole game has changed. And in many countries the governments have changed, and, at least nominally, their political policies have altered. The political watchwords from the Bank and the donor community (but repeated religiously in official Africa) are democracy, decentralisation and participation. The connection between rural development and political form is no longer taboo. The importance of rural community practice has entered the discussion both in its political and its economic dimensions. In this connection the question becomes critical whether de-nationalisation means individual land tenure or community tenure and community management. But the problematics of rural inequities, and the possibility that rural community management might make social asymmetries worse, not better, and might interfere with land tenure policy, is still not fully integrated into the discussion.

As the case history of Sophia shows, people operating in local social systems often reconfigure the effect of national legislation. That lesson can be repeated many times from the Sahelian evidence. State hatched, or internationally hatched, plans to direct local systems along prescribed paths often have had unexpected outcomes. I shall give two examples of efforts to distribute newly available lands in the Sahel. One concerns the irrigation projects in the valley of the Senegal River [*Crousse, Mathieu and Seck (eds.), 1991*]. The other has to do with land made available for human habitation by the eradication of onchocerciasis in the river basins of Burkina Faso [*McMillan, Nana and Savadogo, 1990*].

The irrigation projects on the banks of the Senegal River were variously set up from about the mid-1970s on. In many localities administrators tried to give equal access to newly irrigated lands along the river. As things developed, about half of the inhabitants of the Senegal River Valley had access to irrigated lands at the perimeters of their villages. At first, in many places, the farmers were organised in community groups to participate in and manage these projects. Everyone in the village who wanted to join was to have equal access and a plot of equal size. The whole was to be managed collectively. In fact, in many groups, the principle of equality was violated from the start, with parcels allocated to the names of dead persons, or absent ones [*Mathieu, 1990: 73; 1991: 197*]. These fraudulently registered parcels were in fact controlled by some members of the traditional local elite, and others who were officials or merchants, and counted as *nouveaux riches* [*Mathieu, 1990; Niasse, 1991*]. Some of these were able to use hired labour and to cultivate at a profit.

However, the more impoverished cultivators did badly. They had difficulty maintaining their irrigation channels. They could not recruit the necessary labour from their families, among other things because young men preferred to leave to enter the migrant labour stream. Besides, little by little, from 1985 on, because of international pressure, the state tried to disengage itself from the costs of the inputs (fertilisers, pump maintenance, etc.) and to pass these costs on to the peasantry. The peasants, in turn, borrowed money, mortgaged their parcels, and soon lost their land to the wealthier owners from whom they had received their loans. What is particularly interesting about this example of economic differentiation is that the original economic differences in producer relations were transfers of advantage either from prior social systems, or from new economic and administrative roles. Over time, the profit from the agriculture and the loans intensified the asymmetries, but this was a secondary development. As Mathieu remarked, the state had a very limited margin of manoeuvre, caught as it was between the constraints of international finance and local practices [*Mathieu, 1991: 213*].

The second example of foiled large scale planning that I shall mention was one that took place in Burkina Faso, where 80 per cent of the territory fell within the river basin area of the Onchocerciasis Control Programme [*McMillan et al., 1990: xvii*]. It was an area that might have been suitable for irrigated farming, but which was sparsely populated because of disease, lack of drinking water and various other problems. Spraying was started. It was successful and largely eliminated the parasite. An agency was created to control the anticipated immigration into the area. It was called The Volta Valley Authority (AVV, *Amenagements des Vallées des Volta*). However, to cut a long story short, their design of model settlements, roads and services could be applied only in a limited region, because as soon as the word got out that these lands were now habitable, immense waves of migrants from a variety of ethnic groups simply moved in. They did not wait for the special programmes that had been designed to be put in place. A dignified distinction was made in the official report on this process between sponsored and 'spontaneous' migration. But all did not end well. The report says:

> The continuous stream of immigration, coupled with the extensive cultivation practices used by most migrants is putting stress on area soils. Planners are especially concerned about the steady decline in soil fertility due to decreases in soil organic matter. More intensive cultivation practices, using manure and the reincorporation of crop residues, have enjoyed limited success. Policymakers believe that because the migrants had insecure land rights, they tended to farm the largest area possible rather than adopt more intensive soil conservation practices' [*McMillan, 1990: xxii*] (see also pp.xxxiii and xxxiv).

Land nationalisation was only one dimension of insecurity. There also were major questions about the land interests of the indigenous population. The autochthonous residents had allowed the migrants easy access to the lands for cultivation, but these transactions were understood by them to be loans; temporary grants, not permanent, nor heritable ones. Or at least that is what was being said by local people in retrospect. Conflict was on the horizon. Thus another set of centrally planned interventions was redirected by local events.

But the discourse about how to revise land tenure law does not focus on the implications of such redirections, perhaps because it embraces them. It is evident that the World Bank solution, individual private property and the market, will exacerbate economic and political inequalities, but to the advocates of this position, economic development is the value with the highest priority and inequality is a price worth paying. This clashes with the ideal which others espouse, namely, that land reform should be used as a means of promoting democracy and social justice, of empowering sectors of the population who heretofore have been excluded from political decision-making and economic benefits, and who are now claiming rights they have been denied [*Thomson and Coulibaly, 1994; Thomson, 1994*].

The communitarians, such as Thomson and Coulibaly, argue that land tenure reform can and should be used in the service of greater equality, economic and political. Their conception of social justice is clearly based on an ideal model of gender equality and democratic opportunity. But how communal self-governance can be assumed to guarantee such an objective has not been made clear by its proponents. When community management is idealised, what is swept under the rug is the extent to which existing communities in Africa have themselves been the sites of inequalities and the instigators of exclusions

In a great deal of the discourse about land rights and democracy in the Sahel, the rhetorical preoccupation today is with the excluded, the disenfranchised, the discriminated against. In most areas women do the agricultural work but have no access to a disposable interest in land, and no access to the income from their labours. As the largest group among the deprived, women have become the turning point of the rhetoric of injustice. But women are not the only excluded population. Depending upon which local system one is examining, one can find others equally excluded. The needs of the pastoralists who are denied paths of access to water and pasture for their beasts clash with the needs of cultivators whose fields are trampled on. The descendants of slaves or casted persons are often without civil rights and have no recourse.[4] In many villages, just by reason of age, young men are without power or property.

And last, but by no means least, are the contentious rights of migrants to lands granted to them by the autochthonous residents, and which the autochthones now reclaim. Under conditions of land plenty and an absence of land markets, villagers were often generous. There are many communities in West Africa where 'strangers' who asked to settle locally were offered a plot to cultivate. It is seldom clear under precisely what 'legal' conditions these loans or gifts of land were made. Now all the surrounding circumstances have changed. There has been a dramatic population increase, the population doubling approximately every 25 years. This demographic change combined with chronic drought, increasing aridity, and widespread land degradation has generated a great deal of migration. There are even villages where the im-migrants now heavily outnumber the original population [*Laurent and Mathieu, 1994*]. And in some places the numbers who settle outside their original territories have been augmented by political, refugee-generating disasters. There is no longer a plentiful supply of good land.

One often hears it said that in the past the moral precepts of African culture presupposed that everyone had a *right* to the use of a piece of cultivable land. As Shipton [*1994: 350*] summarised the matter, 'according to this principle, access to land should go to those who need and can use it, and no one should starve for special want of it'. Under the same principle, 'strangers' or 'migrants' who ask for permission to cultivate should not be refused if there is sufficient land to share with them. What happens afterwards depends on local contingencies. As Elias said about African Customary Law:

Of course, the use of land can be transferred temporarily or permanently, as when immigrant settlers are allowed to settle on family land, at first conditionally upon proving in the course of time to be satisfactory components of the host community, and later absolutely upon virtual absorption by and complete assimilation with the landowning groups [*Elias, 1956: 162*].

But the question whether this was a matter of right remains? Was there ever such a *right* in the rule-minded, legal, human rights sense of today? Or are we talking about the frequent *practice* of generosity in the presence of land plenty, the helping of strangers having been at one time an affordable moral ideal.

In many parts of West Africa today, land shortage and conflict over 'rights' to land are major social problems. This is occurring in a geographical area beset by periodic drought, chronic aridity, degradation of the soil, and demographic pressure from a rapidly increasing population. In many parts of the region this has resulted in significant migrations. As migrants move into other people's fallow or into any land that is newly made viable, the potential for conflict increases, whatever the actual circumstances that initially led the migrants to cultivate in other's territory. Governments want to settle the question of who has a right to what. They often think in terms of cadastral surveys and boundary maps, and they are encouraged by the conditionalities of

IMF and World Bank interventions, to think of the goal as one of individual private property in land. But who has the greater right, the original inhabitants or the needy migrants? Do both have legitimate claims? Who is to decide that question and who is to enforce the decision?

THE WAY THINGS ARE: RIGHTS, CLAIMS AND, PERHAPS, REMEDIES

There is a striking difference between two of the many currents of talk about rights. One concerns what 'should be' and the other concerns 'what is'. One is located in the theoretical debates that surround the worldwide human rights movement, the other in the reports of anthropologists who describe people who are actually claiming rights in the course of managing their affairs. Transcendant moral, legal and cultural criteria occupy the theorists. Their question is: what would an abstract and portable international definition of human rights be, one that might serve as a standard anywhere? By contrast, anthropologists are concerned with the actual life situation of particular people at a particular time and place, people who formulate some of their problems in terms of what they see as their rights, their due. The difference I want to emphasise between the grand talk of what 'should be' and the particularistic accounts of 'what is', is not the distinction between universalism and relativism which is so tirelessly (and often fruitlessly) discussed in the human rights literature. What I want to emphasise is the difference in political subtext between these two perspectives.

The philosophically-minded human rights advocates, social theorists, lawyers and others, set their agenda in an international political arena. They think in terms of international law. They want to transcend all parochialisms to make their case, to mobilise worldwide support for a set of ideals on a transnational basis, hoping that local applications will ensue. It is a top/down perspective. The legalistic definitions that are sought are absolute. One either has a declared right or does not. The rights are entitlements that go with the condition of being human.

This broad international discourse on human rights runs on a track parallel to many other international communications and contacts (see Merry [1992] for a bibliographical overview of the anthropological literature on transnational processes). It intersects with social theory and philosophical thought about the human condition, and it also has links with international organisations and with activist political causes.

The anthropologist may have such connections as well. But the strength of the fieldwork perspective is that anthropology provides a specific description of 'what is' happening on the ground at a particular time and place. This includes, to the extent that such is possible, tracing the impact on the social field studied of official interventions, economic upheavals, and the contact with a continuously changing traffic in ideas.

Much is likely to manifest itself indirectly. In that regard, among the most revealing events in the observable scene are likely to be the small-scale contestations over rights that take place between rival claimants. These minor struggles, and the justifications they invoke, expose the dynamics and culture of a wider political arena. Anthropology, to the extent that it considers the future by looking at the present, can give the lofty transnational discourse on moral principles and legal doctrines a distinct whiff of the practical and the possible. Anthropology is positioned to press the question, 'How do you get from here to there?'

Thus, precisely because land problems, and the reform of systems of land tenure, engage with all of these complex issues at many levels, and are nothing if they are not practical problems, they are a useful route through which to think about human rights in Africa [An-Na'im and Deng, 1990: 218, 245]. There is no situation that brings African political incapacities to the surface more clearly. African states are often confronted with land problems they cannot or will not handle. There are serious questions involved about law, about rights, about the dignity and well-being of human beings.

Human rights, in the strictest, recent, international law sense, began with protections of the rights of individual persons in relation to governments. As an overarching body, the international community of states has collectively committed itself to many such protections, and to doing what it can to see that states honour them [Henkin, 1981; 1994]. But states often disregard their commitments in this regard and much of the time the international community does not have the will or the capacity to enforce the commitments that were made. Thus, even to the extent they are clear, the certainties of legal rights are not matched by practical measures for the legal recognition of violations and the enforcement of norms. This has been very extensively remarked on in the African context [Cohen, Hyden and Nagan, 1993; AnNa'im and Deng, 1990]; see also Messer [1993] in an overview of anthropology and human rights).

But whatever the actual complexities and practical limitations on the implementation of human rights as iterated in international law, there is no such limitation on discussing an expanded moral vision of what human entitlements ought to be. 'Human rights are among the few utopian ideals left' [Wilson, 1997: 1]. But, in fact, the possibility of making them operational may be the crucial question.

When one comes to consider land problems in Africa one is obliged to think not just about what is desirable, but rather about what is possible, where and when. Nor can the blame for every trouble be placed on the state. From the point of view of the victims of events of land deprivation, the ultimate results of very different causes may seem the same. The confiscation of land without compensation by a government, the seizure of land by a powerful individual, or by a rival ethnic group, or a major interference with beneficial use by competitors, or the experience of being driven away by land degradation and drought, all end in deprivation.[5]

The course of capitalist development itself may drive rural people from their land. In West Africa one recent report argued that urban activities are more 'productive' than rural activities, hence that investment should go to urban rather than rural areas. The thesis of the report was that the city is the motor of development. It argued that urban growth stimulates production in the countryside. The general prediction was that the sooner that 'unproductive', barely surviving small-holders were pushed off their land by the action of the market, the sooner that economically efficient agro-businesses would be able to take over and make the countryside more productive [Cour, 1995]. That study implies that the small-holders would then become labourers in the rural areas or join the urban poor in the informal economy. Such development visions of the future can scarcely reassure rural holders. Happily there are critiques that contest some of this analysis [D'Agostino, 1995; Dione, 1995; Reardon and Staatz, 1995].

As far as the logic of a rural agricultural population of smallholders is concerned, if you do not have a piece of productive land you do not have food, and you and your family may die. The right to life in an agrarian society can be conceived as the right to access to land and all the inputs, such as water, necessary to make it minimally productive. Hence for rural agriculturalists, the most urgent issue is not about human rights as a conception, but about survival in the here and now, and to whom to turn for some guarantee of security. It is obvious that there can be more than one claimant for a piece of land, and more than one entity that wants to control the use of land. Who is to judge which claims are legitimate, and what settlements are fair?

Whatever the particular details that precede a loss, there is seldom a neutral forum to which small-holders who anticipate being expropriated or pushed out can present their dilemmas. There is no political arena where they have standing and can communicate their case in advance of loss. However clearly Jürgen Habermas [1996: 122–31] can imagine democratic fora where the moral value of alternatives might be freely and fairly debated, there are usually no such fora for these issues. For example, there is no place where international development agencies and the target populations of particular development programmes can have a debate about the issues and policies under conditions of democratic equality.

Besides, moral values, even when agreed upon, may not be sufficient to solve practical problems. Rival populations claiming the same lands, both having good grounds for their claims, may need matters to be resolved by supervised negotiation, or by some other means such as resettlement programmes. There may be a need for large scale plans which provide alternative options where accommodating both sets of legitimate claimants is physically impossible. Agencies are needed which can ascertain the legitimacy of claims, and then address them without being confined to a legalistic, adversarial, either/or solution.

Conditions vary. To match them, remedial possibilities must vary. Further, when the direct agency of deprivation is not the state, what follows? Is the state to be held responsible in human rights doctrine for not intervening when there are violations of land rights by one ethnic group against another within its borders? (And when the state is a suspected accomplice of such appropriations as recently in Kenya, what then?) Should state responsibility under human rights doctrines be extended to deprivations due to environmental damage? Should the state (or multi-state regional bodies) be responsible for looking after populations that have been driven out of their territories by aridity or land degradation? Or by the workings of the economy?

Human rights discussions in the abstract, with an emphasis on what is morally desirable, seem quite aimless without a concomitant discussion of the practical conditions under which action could be taken. It seems necessary to ask why there is such a paucity of effective agencies of recognition, debate and redress. Without a discussion of the political preconditions involved in meeting the human rights agenda, there is little headway to be made.

It is my view that without some attention to practical institutional possibilities from the start, there are no legal rights to discuss, only moral claims and responsive sympathies. Rights without remedies are ephemeral. To ask how to create an appropriate space where legitimate claims could be acknowledged and acted upon is very much to the point. Such practical and pragmatic questions must go in tandem with any discussion of what constitutes a right. Posing the questions may do no more than show that at a particular place and time no morally satisfactory solutions could possibly be realised. It may sometimes be necessary to be willing to acknowledge incapacity.

The practical and operational sides of rights questions should not be ignored. Anthropology is particularly well placed to contribute to that aspect of the discussion. Such practical issues are bound to lead beyond the consolations found in the high-sounding normative statements of international treaties, and beyond the idealistic discourse of a benign philosophical morality. They lead to a knowledge of nasty politics, vicious and violent competitions, and perhaps even to serious reflections on existing economic and political inequities. What would the preconditions be for better possibilities to emerge? That is the question that should be asked more often. If legal and moral human rights talk ultimately leads to such reflections it is a good thing. But by itself, it is not enough.

NOTES

1. See James [*1971*] for a review of Tanzanian land law as of the date of publication; and James and Fimbo [*1973*] and Moore [*1986*].
2. APREFA, Association pour la promotion des recherches et études foncieres en Afrique; for Le Roy's view, see Le Roy [*1996: 10–12*].
3. See Finnemore [*1997*] on a sequence of World Bank redefinitions of development.
4. See van Dijk [*1996: 30*] on the exclusion of the descendants of slaves from desirable land near a new well in Mali.
5. See Faure [*1997*] on confiscation without compensation in Burkina Faso; and Nowrojee [*1993: 19ff., 49–93*] on ethnic violence, land appropriation and government involvement in arming the aggressors in the Rift Valley of Kenya; also note the examples of migration cited earlier here.

REFERENCES

An-Na'im, Abdullah Ahmed and Francis Deng (eds.), 1990, *Human Rights in Africa*, Washington, DC: The Brookings Institution.
Cohen, Ronald, Hyden, Göran and Winston P. Nagan (eds.), 1993, *Human Rights and Governance in Africa*, Gainesville, FL: University Press of Florida.
Crousse, Bernard, Mathieu, Paul and Sidy M. Seck (eds.), 1991, *La Vallée du Fleuve Senegal*, Paris: Karthala.
Cour, Jean-Marie (Director of Study), 1995, *West Africa Long Term Perspective Study (WALTPS)*, carried out by Cinergie Unit of African Development Bank (Abidjan), Secretariat of the Club du Sahel of the OECD (Paris) and CILSS (Ouagadougou), Summary Report, SAH/D(94)439, Paris.
Dijk, Han van, 1996, 'Land tenure, Territoriality and Ecological Instability', in Joep Spiertz and Melanie G. Wiber (eds.), *The Role of Law in Natural Resource Management*, The Hague: VUGA.
D'Agostino, Victoire, 1995, 'Notes on the WALTPS: points of agreement and disagreement', unpublished internal memorandum, Club du Sahel.
Dione, Josue, 1995, 'Comments on the WALTPS Results and Implications,' *MSU/INSAH-PRISAS*, Food Security Briefing Paper, No.95-02.
Elias, T. Olawale, 1956, *The Nature of African Customary Law*, Manchester: Manchester University Press.
Ellickson, Robert C., 1991, *Order without Law*, Cambridge, MA: Harvard University Press.
Faure, Armelle, 1995, 'Private Land Ownership in Rural Burkina Faso', International Institute for Environment and Development Paper, No.59, October.
Faure, Armelle, 1997, 'Le droit des ruraux en cas de perte du foncier, l'exemple du Burkina Faso,' paper presented at the 'Colloque International sur le Foncier au Sahel', Université de Saint Louis, Sénégal, 21–25 April.
Finnemore, Martha, 1997, 'Redefining Development at the World Bank', in Frederick Cooper and Randall Packard (eds.), *International Development and the Social Sciences*, Berkeley, CA: University of California Press.
Habermas, Jürgen, 1996, *Between Facts and Norms*, (translated by William Rehg), Cambridge, MA: MIT Press.
Henkin, Louis (ed.), 1981, *The International Bill of Rights*, New York: Columbia University Press.
Henkin, Louis (ed.), 1994, *Human Rights: An Agenda for the Next Century*, Washington, DC: American Society of International Law.
Hesseling, Gerti and Boubakar Moussa Ba (with the collaboration of Paul Mathieu, Mark S. Freudenberger, Samba Soumare), 1994, *Land Tenure and Natural Resource Management in the Sahel*, CILSS (Permanent Inter-State Committee for Drought Control in the Sahel), OECD (Organisation for Economic Co-operation and Development) and Club du Sahel.
Hohfeld, Wesley Newcomb, 1919, *Fundamental Legal Conceptions as Applied in Judicial Reasoning*, New Haven, CT: Yale University Press.
James, R.W., 1971, *Land Tenure and Policy in Tanzania*, Nairobi/Dar es Salaam/Kampala: East African Literature Bureau.

James, R.W. and G.M. Fimbo, 1973, *Customary Land Law of Tanzania*, Nairobi/Kampala/Dar es Salaam: East African Literature Bureau.

Laurent, Pierre Joseph and Paul Mathieu, 1994, 'Authority and Conflict in the Management of Natural Resources', in Henrik Secher Marcussen (ed.), *Improved Natural Resource Management: The Role of the State versus that of the Local Community*, Occasional Paper No.12, International Development Studies, Roskilde University, Roskilde, Denmark.

Le Roy, Etienne, Karsenty, Alain and Alain Bertrand (eds.), 1996, *La securisation fonciere en Afrique*, Paris: Karthala.

Low, D.A., 1996, *The Egalitarian Moment*, Cambridge: Cambridge University Press.

McMillan, Della, Nana, Jean-Baptiste and Kimseyinga Savadogo, 1990, 'Settlement Experiences and Development Strategies in the Onchocerciasis Control Programme Areas of West Africa, Country Case Study: Burkina Faso', mimeo.

Mamdani, Mahmood, 1996, *Citizen and Subject: Contemporary Africa and the Legacy of Late Colonialism*, Princeton, NJ: Princeton University Press.

Mathieu, Paul, 1990, 'Usages de la loi et pratiques foncieres dans les amenagements irrigues', *Politique Africaine*, No.40, pp.72-81.

Mathieu, Paul, 1991, 'Irrigation, transformation economique et enjeux fonciers', in Crousse, Mathieu and Seck [*1991*].

Merry, Sally, 1992, 'Anthropology, Law and Transnational Processes,' *Annual Review of Anthropology*, Vol.21, pp.357-79.

Messer, Ellen, 1993, 'Anthropology and Human Rights', *Annual Review of Anthropology*, Vol.22, pp.221-49.

Moore, Sally Falk, 1977, 'Political Meetings and the Simulation of Unanimity: Kilimanjaro, 1973', in S.F. Moore and B. Myerhoff (eds.), *Secular Ritual*, Assen: Van Gorcum.

Moore, Sally Falk, 1986, *Social Facts and Fabrications: 'Customary Law' on Kilimanjaro 1880–1980*, Cambridge: Cambridge University Press.

Moore, Sally Falk, 1987, 'Explaining the Present: Theoretical Dilemmas in Processual Ethnography', *American Ethnologist*, Vol.14, No.4.

Moore, Sally Falk, 1993, 'The Ethnography of the Present and the Analysis of Process', in Robert Borofsky (ed.), *Assessing Cultural Anthropology*, New York: McGraw-Hill.

Niasse, Madodio, 1991, 'Les perimetres irrigues villageois vieillissent mal', in Crousse, Mathieu and Seck [*1991*].

Nowrojee, Binaifer, 1993, *Divide and Rule: State Sponsored Ethnic Violence in Kenya*, Africa Watch, New York/ Washington/ Los Angeles/ London.

Reardon, Thomas and John M. Staatz, 1995, 'Reflections on WALTPS Results and Recommendations', MSU/INSAH-PRISAS Food Security Briefing Paper, No.95-02.

Scott, James C., 1998, *Seeing Like a State*, New Haven, CT and London: Yale University Press.

Shipton, Parker, 1994, 'Land and Culture in Tropical Africa', *Annual Review of Anthropology*, Vol.23, pp.347-77.

Simon, Herbert, 1957, 'Rationality and Administrative Decision Making', in *Models of Man*, London and New York: John Wiley.

Thomson, James and Cheibane Coulibaly, 1994, *Decentralization in the Sahel*, CILSS (Permanent Interstate Committee for Drought Control in the Sahel), OECD (Organization for Economic Cooperation and Development) and Club du Sahel.

Thomson, James T., 1994, 'The Role of the State versus the Community in Governance and Management of Renewable Natural Resources', in Marcussen, Henrik Secher (ed.), *Improved Natural Resource Management: The Role of the State versus that of the Local Community*, Occasional Paper No.12, International Development Studies, Roskilde University, Roskilde, Denmark.

Wilson, Richard A. (ed.), 1997, *Human Rights, Culture and Context*, London: Pluto Press.

Politics and Struggles for Access to Land: 'Grants from Above' and 'Squatters' in Coastal Kenya

KARUTI KANYINGA

In Kenya and sub-Saharan Africa generally, there has been little systematic discussion of post-colonial struggles for land rights. Studies have ignored the fact that the 'land question' is not about production alone and have, thus, failed to assess its wider consequences for society. This raises questions about the current socio-political dimension of the land question and the consequences of the interplay between the 'land question' and other changes under way in the country. This study addresses these questions by discussing popular struggles of access to land in the coastal region of Kenya where the land question has a distinct political history. The analysis is based on a survey conducted in Kilifi district, Coast provinces, between September 1995 and November 1996.

INTRODUCTION

Until recently, academic interest in the question of access to and struggles around land ownership in sub-Saharan Africa, what is now known as 'the land question', centred around land tenure reforms and agricultural production. Discussions have routinely ignored the fact that the land question comprises several aspects and cannot be reduced to the issue of agricultural development alone: the land question is also at the centre of the social and political organisation of agrarian social formations. This is apparently responsible for the resurgence of the land question in economic, political and social discourse and, particularly, in the constitution engineering processes in a majority of sub-Saharan African countries. Of concern is that 'economic reductionism' in the conventional literature tended to regard private property in land as a necessary condition for the development of capital accumulation in agrarian

Karuti Kanyinga, Research Fellow, Institute for Development Studies, University of Nairobi, Kenya. The author is currently based at the Centre for Development Research, Copenhagen, and is finalising his Ph.D. on Land and Politics in Kenya at the Roskilde University Centre, Denmark. The author wishes to thank the Nordic African Institute, Uppsala, for financing the study on which this contribution is based.

societies, on the assumption that this would provide security for investment which would, in turn, boost agricultural production on which the continent's economy depends. This thinking reflects, not surprisingly, the World Bank's sectoral work and Structural Adjustment Programmes: the Bank has been supporting titling efforts on the assumption that this will ensure secure land rights, activate markets and increase agricultural production [*World Bank, 1989; Platteau, 1996*].

Generally speaking, there are fewer contemporary studies of the political aspects of the land question compared to the colonial period where considerable attention was given to 'land-based' peasant resistance movements in 'colonies' where a settler economy dominated. Studies have not paid much attention to the socio-political aspects of the land question in the post-colonial period, yet the land question continues to inform the organisation of local and national politics in these societies. Moreover, recent years have witnessed the reactivation of ethnic sub-nationalism in the continent, much of which is reinforced by quests for control of certain ethno-territorial claims which now tend to be the main challenge to the nation-state project in Africa.

The significance of the land question in African societies is bound to increase for the land question is embedded in a dynamic and a broad social political context [*Basset and Crummey, 1993; Berry, 1993: 101–34*]. It also has a bearing on patterns of social relations in the society. How land is held, and specifically how 'access to land' is regulated, are dimensions of importance to the organisation of economics and politics of that particular social formation [*Njeru, 1978; Glazier, 1985: 3–10; Mamdani, 1996: 109–22*]. Any changes in the structure of land ownership has consequences for the socio-political aspects of that particular society and not only for its structure of agricultural development [*Okoth-Ogendo, 1979: 152–3; 1991*]. Where studies have attempted to redress this imbalance, the result has been a tendency towards 'moralisation' and/or idealisation of customary land tenure regimes.

This study attempts to go beyond both the 'economic reductionism fashion' and the 'moralised' customary tenure regime by discussing the land question within a broader socio-political and economic context. The discussion builds around the questions 'what are the current socio-political dimensions to the land question and what is the consequence of their interplay with other changes under way in the continent?' The discussion teases out socio-political relations that lie beneath property rights in land with a view to highlighting other issues pertinent to the land question debate. It deals with several case studies on struggles for land rights in Coastal Kenya where the land question has a long and distinct political history from the up-country one about which much has been written. The study is based on the findings of a survey conducted in Kilifi District, Coast Province, between September 1995 and November 1996.

A case study on Kenya – and on the coastal region of that country – is particularly instructive because the land reform programme in Kenya has been quite comprehensive and has been at the centre of national political and economic events. Land reform began during the colonial period as a result of a report on how 'to Intensify the Development of African Agriculture in Kenya' prepared in 1954 by the then Deputy Director of Agriculture, R.J.M. Swynnerton. The Swynnerton Plan aimed to displace indigenous land tenure systems and impose private property rights along the lines of English land law [*Swynnerton, 1954*]. The Plan thus sought to re-configure the context of land rights by imposing alien laws on property rights in land. This had severe consequences not only for the existing tenure regime but also for the organisation of society in general.

   Along the coast, and particularly along the ten-mile coastal strip (Mwambao) which was under the 'suzerainty' of the Sultan of Zanzibar, problems around control and ownership of land have roots in the pre-colonial situation. The land question was formulated here after the Arabs and the Swahili settled in the area, consolidated the slave trade and then gained control of the land. The colonial state deepened the problem by introducing legislation which entitled only the subjects of the Sultan (comprising mainly Arabs and the Swahili Muslims) to register land as private property [*Ghai and McAuslan, 1970: 29; Charo, 1977; Cooper, 1980*]. The post-colonial state worsened the problem by giving grants of land to politicians even in areas already occupied by the indigenous Mijikenda groups. This resulted in increasing landlessness and squatter problems.

POLITICS AND LAND RIGHTS IN KENYA

Kenya's land question in general has roots in the colonial situation and was shaped by three distinct but interrelated processes [*Sorrenson, 1967; 1968; Okoth Ogendo, 1979; 1987; 1991*]. The first, from which others followed, was alienation and acquisition of land as a prelude to the establishment of a colonial state. The sequel to this was the imposition of English property law and its acclamation of title and private property rights in the alienated areas. Land tenure reform in the Native Reserves under the Swynnerton Plan completed the question by both deepening and diversifying its structure. Each of these processes gave rise to unique but related sets of problems regarding access and control of land, thereby laying the basis for a rather 'complex land question' whose solution continues to plague the Kenyan polity. This had several consequences. First, the processes caused mass displacement in alienated areas and especially among the Kikuyu of Central Kenya. It gave rise to a mass of people without land rights – the squatters. The Swynnerton Plan restructured the property rights system and thereby affected the social organisation of the society. One immediate response was the consolidation of a peasant rebellion – the Mau Mau – organised especially by those who had lost rights to land through the imposed property rights system.

The squatter problem later became the basis for the organisation of a peasant rebellion – the Mau Mau – against the colonial state; the rebellion aimed for *Uhuru* (independence) which they thought would result in the return of the 'stolen' land. Secondly, alienation contributed to the 'ethnicisation' of the land question: the squatters moved into the Rift Valley where they sold labour to the colonial settlers and swelled the numbers of displaced ethnic groups, such as the Kalenjin and the Maasai. Consequently, ethnic tension over the control of land in the area deepened in tandem with the consolidation of the struggle for *Uhuru*. Some of these other groups feared that the squatters would accede to land rights in the former settler areas and deny them control of what they considered to be their 'tribal' spheres. They consequently began to fence off the squatters from the region and in some cases violently evicted them.

In addition to the reform of land tenure in the reserves, in the 1960s the government introduced a parallel programme for 're-Africanisation' in the White Highlands, previously 'scheduled' for European settlement. This aimed to alter the racial structure of land ownership and to address the ethnic and political dimensions of the land question complex. The government established several settlement schemes for the landless and introduced a land purchase programme for the African middle class to accede to the 'scheduled areas' [*Leys, 1975; Njonjo, 1978; Leo, 1985*].

Both the reform of land tenure and the 're-Africanisation' programme had a profound effect on the nation-building project; they considerably shaped the politics of transition and have continued to shape local and wider politics. Notably, at the time of transition to independence, the land question directly influenced the debate on the form of constitutional and economic arrangements and later the formation of political parties [*Bates, 1989: 46–50; Harbeson, 1973: 81–134*]. The parties formed to participate in the politics of transition constructed a distinct answer to the land question as a means of negotiating independence with the colonial government following the defeat of the Mau Mau peasant rebellion.

The two main parties were the Kenya African National Union (KANU) and the Kenya African Democratic Union (KADU). KANU, an alliance of two numerically large groups – the Kikuyu and the Luo – preferred a centralised state and unitary form of government and emphasised respect for private property rights. It also had on its board a radical nationalist faction which advocated *Nyakua* (forcible seizure) of expropriated land in line with the need to reward Mau Mau freedom fighters. KADU, formed out of an amalgamation of smaller groups – the Kalenjin, Maasai, Turkana, and the Samburu (KAMATUSA), the Somalia and the Mijikenda among others – fearing domination by the Kikuyu and Luo, preferred a federal system of government (Majimbo) with regional assemblies whose most significant duty would be the administration of land matters. KADU saw this as a check on the land-hungry Kikuyu squatters who were already settled in the white highlands to which KAMATUSA had historical territorial claims. The settlers also formed the New Kenya Party to protect and preserve their interests in land. Their party later allied with KADU to push for federalism and respect of land rights as advocated by KADU leaders.

KANU won the elections in 1961 and 1963 and formed a government of influential liberal politicians, led by Kenyatta and Tom Mboya, who articulated the demand for a unitary form of government and respect for private land rights wherever established. KADU was dissolved in 1964 in the 'national interest' and KANU accommodated its leaders including those who advocated preservation of 'ethno-territorial land claims'. This eroded the influence of the radicals in KANU as they could no longer threaten to defect and temporarily 'froze' the land question, its ethnic dimension being replaced by a class-based politics of access to and control of the land.

The liberals in KANU and in particular those who constituted the inner court for the first government (the Kenyatta administration) were keen not to disturb the legal framework on economic development laid down by the colonial state. They were convinced that consolidating property rights in land would lead to intensified agricultural productivity on which the economy depended. The conflict over land and the manner in which it was resolved thus had two important consequences. First, a constitutional arrangement evolved that favoured sanctity and inviolability of private property rights and provided protection from deprivation of property without compensation. Second, it resulted in the wholesale adoption of the legal framework on which the colonial reform of land tenure had depended. These outcomes, and the protection of private property in particular, encouraged unlimited accumulation of land in the 'scheduled' areas by the liberals in KANU and KADU as fears of confiscation by radicals were allayed.

The accession of Daniel Arap Moi to the Presidency, following the death of Kenyatta in 1978, saw a 'thawing' of the land question. Moi was one of the senior KADU leaders who had vehemently advocated federalism (Majimbo) to protect the land and political rights of smaller agro-pastoralist communities against the large ethnic groups. His presidency saw a reconstitution of former KADU elites; their 'ideology on land' soon becoming the focus of politics and the state itself. At the same time, it aroused high expectations among the KAMATUSA groups who subsequently fenced off their areas, closing the frontiers in the Rift Valley where land hungry groups had migrated to acquire land. In relation to this, to construct an independent base of political support, Moi ordered rapid individualisation of farms owned by land buying groups (co-operatives and companies and partnerships) and subsequent registration of titles for individual shareholders.

Simultaneous with the closing of the frontiers, political patronage evolved as the single most important medium of regulating access to public land. The government continued to reward political clients with land with a view to establishing a stable political and economic class. From the early 1990s, with increasing pressures for political liberalisation, the pace of appropriation of government land by political elites increased as Moi struggled to retain loyalists, a clientele that was otherwise rapidly disintegrating.

As pressure for political liberalisation deepened, the KADU group, hitherto constituting KANU leadership, began to appropriate the land question for a different but related political project. They used the 'thawing land question' as a tool to fight their political opponents, in the belief that multi-partyism implied the end of the Moi leadership. This resulted in ethnic land clashes between members of former KADU groups and the immigrant population in the Rift Valley and, much later, on the Coast between the Mijikenda and upcountry Kikuyu and Luo immigrants. KANU won the 1992 elections but left behind a simmering land question, an issue that has continued to influence political developments in the country. The Rift Valley and areas around the Coast have witnessed the most violent and unprecedented ethnic conflicts in recent years. Although some conflicts are expressed in the form of party politics they have their logic in the 'thawing' land question. The following section examines the evolution of the land question in the Coastal area and examines its implications for local and wider politics.

THE COASTAL LAND QUESTION

As mentioned earlier, the land question on the coast arose in tandem with the consolidation of both the slave trade and 'Sultan rule' on the Coast. The entry of the British administration deepened it in two significant ways. First, the rivalry between the British and Germans over the control of the East African coast resulted in the two 'awarding' the Sultan 'sovereign rights' over a 10 mile coastal strip – Mwambao. This allowed the Sultan's subjects to have private property in land but denied this right to the indigenous inhabitants because they were not subjects of the Sultan and/or were not Muslims [*Republic of Kenya, 1978*]. Second, the British promulgated a law in 1908, the Land Titles Ordinance, which enabled the colonial authorities to determine the extent of private possessions before they could alienate land for the Crown and/or give grants to individual settlers. This also enabled the British administration to penetrate and control the interior. This Ordinance, and its version of land tenure on the coast, began by altering the distribution of land first among the Arabs and the Swahili. The Ordinance then closed off avenues through which the indigenous Mijikenda and ex-slaves could have made claims to land on the coastal belt. Instead the administration introduced 'Native Reserves', removing indigenous people from certain areas in order to make way for European settlement.

The evolution of the land question on the coast entered a new phase with the negotiations for political independence in the wider colony. At the time of transition to independence, the British government entered into a pre-independence agreement with the Kenyatta administration and the Sultan regarding control of land in Mwambao [*Salim, 1968: 224; Ghai and MacAuslan, 1970: 187–8*]. Kenyatta conceded the Sultan's demands for recognition of private land rights on the 'Coast' and promised to adjudicate and register such rights where they were not adjudicated, notwithstanding the negated land rights of the indigenous groups. Both the agreement and negotiations over independence concluded the process of creating the squatter phenomenon: they transformed the Mijikenda into squatters or 'tenants of the Arabs and the Swahili landowners'.

The first government thenceforth favoured private property rights irrespective of how they had been acquired. The government also acknowledged the problem of landlessness on the coast and appointed two different committees at different times between the late 1960s and the mid 1970s to advise on how to resolve the problem. With regard to the squatters, the government favoured establishing various schemes on former Crown lands (now government land) or on land purchased from those who were willing to sell. It was hoped that these schemes would solve landlessness and safeguard the principle of private landownership both of which would help circumvent possible invasion of private land by squatters. Much later, in the early 1970s, the government also began a programme of individualisation – land tenure reform – arguing that the communal manner in which land was held was a canopy of landlessness on the coast and that unless land was individualised 'the government would neither know the magnitude of the problem nor would holders effectively utilize their holdings'. None of these approaches effectively tackled the land problems on the coast: instead they engendered different sorts of reform and thereby complicated the land question as argued below.

Case 1: Politics of Resettlement Efforts

Economic and political rationale guided the establishment of settlement schemes on the Coast. The government saw in the schemes opportunities for peasants to participate in agricultural production and thereby increase production in the sector. Post-independence pressure from radical politicians underpinned the political rationale. This led to the government establishing settlement schemes for the landless to prevent violent political conflicts between the Coastal landless, on the one hand, and the upcountry settlers and the Arab-Swahili 'landlords' on the other.

These resettlement schemes were not specifically established for the landless in the coast region; upcountry groups obtained land here despite landlessness among the coastal people and the fact that the land question here differed considerably from the upcountry one. Increasing number of 'outsiders' and malpractice in the allocation of plots gradually engendered hostilities between the indigenous groups and the new beneficiaries, with the local people often accusing the local Provincial Administration of 'tantalising' squatters with promises of more land. These promises were rarely fulfilled.

Related to this was the problem of political patronage in allocation of plots in the settlement schemes to elites (through 'grants from above'). In the view of many, officers in the Provincial Administration and upcountry political elites were 'second to Arab and Swahili landowners in acquiring private land rights and titles in the area: they not only "grabbed" land meant for the landless but also invited others to do the same'. This expropriation resulted in less land for resettlement; it added to the mass of people without user rights. The schemes thus could not eliminate or even reduce the problem of landlessness.

These 'grants from above' had another effect: they intensified disputes over control of land in the area and widened divisions between local residents and the new land owners, the state at the local level, officers in the Ministry of Lands and those in the Provincial Administration. Several disputes and conflicts involving local politicians and the indigenous people on one side and the government and upcountry political elites on the other broke out immediately after the schemes started. In Magarini Settlement Scheme Complex started in 1978, for instance, local politicians often complained of biases by settlement officers in the allocation of plots and of evictions of coastal beneficiaries and their replacement with upcountry ones. In 1984 controversy over these allocations reached the floor of parliament where questions and answers were more revealing: senior government officials listed their constituents and friends and recommended them to be given plots by the settlement officers. To avoid embarrassment and possible political backlash, the government emphasised that all land in Kenya was 'national land' on which anyone could be settled irrespective of ethnic identity and that 'Magarini was not a scheme only for the Coastal people' (*Weekly Review,* 4 May 1984). Since then allocation of land on the scheme continued to be the focus of area politics with local politicians mobilising support around promises to ensure that the government would give priority to the local people.

Problems of access to land in the settlement schemes have a longer history as the following case study shows. Some have roots in the 'grants from above' given by the colonial administration but nevertheless have continued to inform the organisation of local politics. In Kijipwa area of Kilifi district, a settler farmer obtained land during the colonial period to experiment with sisal farming. Following on his success, he obtained more land for a plantation. The displaced people moved to neighbouring locations but were evicted again in the late 1960s when the plantation acquired more land including that on which some had settled. This time, however, they resisted eviction and repelled the local Provincial Administration and the owners of the plantation. They won several concessions among which was the authority to occupy the area 'as the government looked for land to settle them' on condition that 'they lived in peace'. They continued to occupy the land and even subdivided it among themselves 'on conviction that they were the rightful owners of the land and that the government would give them secure tenure rights'.

Meanwhile, pressure mounted on local politicians, particularly the then senior and influential cabinet Minister, Ronald Ngala, to petition the government for allocation and for titles to the land occupied by squatters in the coastal region. Ngala received Kenyatta's assurance that a settlement scheme would be established for the squatters and the landless in Kilifi among other areas. Several schemes were established but these were inadequate given the high number of landless people on the coast (estimated in the mid-1970s at about one-quarter of the population). Moreover, the state was increasingly alienating land and turning it over to elites connected to central state politicians. Area residents who had knowledge about these events complained that land for the scheme was set aside in a rocky place and far away from where they had settled. Much later, in 1982, another scheme was established in the area which had been occupied, especially by those who refused to move out after the first wave of eviction.

The whole exercise of resettlement was left in the hands of government officers – the chiefs and the officers in the Department of Settlement – who answered to yet another settlement committee headed by the District Commissioner (DC). These officers subsequently abused the allocation procedures: those families with poor relations with the chiefs or their associates had their names omitted from the list of occupants while 'friends of the officers' had both the 'household heads and eldest sons listed separately as occupants' to increase their chances of getting more than one plot. Other officers also listed names of their relatives and friends who were not residents in the area.

In the actual distribution that followed, fewer people than those initially planned for obtained plots. Some families acquired more than one plot while others had none at all. This was more disappointing for those who had occupied the area from the mid-1960s. They lost not only the holdings but also tree crops and other investments undertaken during their long period of occupancy. Others were unfortunate in other respects – they were allocated land in virgin areas, away from where they had settled and grown tree crops.

Other problems followed. Initially both the demarcation officers in the Ministry of Lands and the local Provincial Administration had announced that the scheme was designed for hundreds of five acre (two hectare) plots, enough for the registered occupants. In fact, the size of the holdings was reduced from five to two and half acres, with those responsible giving the excuse that 'this would enable all the occupants get land'.

This was just a smokescreen for the fact that elites had obtained 'grants from above' which effectively reduced the size of the area destined for the scheme. Several government officials and politically connected individuals who included cabinet Ministers, permanent secretaries (some from the coast), senior officers in the Ministry of Lands and Settlement, a judge, a prominent leader of a national choir group and a District Officer (DO), among others, acquired large portions of land here. Some of these were given land on which squatters lived and cultivated and therefore land on which their livelihood depended. Additionally, the 'plantation had already acquired the other better part'.

Those who lost their land rights took their complaints to the Provincial Administration but no one could interfere with the grants. Most complainants were turned away and told 'to keep peace, for the Nyayo government will solve the plight of the homeless' (*Nyayo* literally means footsteps; it is used to refer to Moi because of his often repeated promise to follow Kenyatta's footsteps). Others were listened to by the District Commissioner but were told that the land now 'belongs to the allottees because they had titles to it'. Aware that they probably would have got land were it not for the huge tracts that had been allocated from above, those who missed the plots refused to give way to the new owners. They hoped that their persistent appeals to the Provincial Administration and local leaders would bear fruits. But some of the land had already changed hands without their knowledge: some of the allottees had already turned over the land to private developers (foreign hoteliers operating in partnership with influential economic elites) who then began to expel the occupants. The bases for another struggle had begun in earnest.

Some of the new owners, impatient with the occupants, brought in bulldozers and flattened the area without a warning to occupants. These evictions did not spread fast, however. Occupants resisted, arguing that 'they had more rights to the land than the allottees and that they should have been given priority in the allocations by virtue of having been the first occupants'. From then on, they began violently to confront the new land owners and keep them at bay. This kept potential buyers away as well.

With the assistance of the new owner, some of the squatters eventually got land far away from the area or went to squat elsewhere. Other allottees were unable to get alternative land for occupants through the Provincial Administration and therefore decided to use the courts claiming that the squatters were 'professional squatters' who had sold their land with a view to politicising the land question on the coast. But rarely did the courts enforce requests for eviction. In several cases the new owners were ordered to give occupants time to look for alternative land.

The resettlement efforts, thus, were not an adequate solution to the land question. They deepened rather than solved it. Economic interests of politically influential elites also deepened the land question. 'Grants from above' resulted in concentrating the best land in the hands of the economic and political elites who turned them over to foreign hoteliers. Their interests were certainly in direct conflict with the survival needs of the peasantry. Perhaps these conflicts over access to land would not have been so intense had the elites managed to provide alternative land to the squatters. The cases also demonstrate the limitations of 'accumulation from above' and political patronage in general. Those affected are able to resist it; to make the machinery for accomplishing political patronage unreliable and ineffective and to generally put such forms of accumulation on hold. 'Accumulation from above' also has its own costs: taking advantage of it incurs costs that not even the politically influential can circumvent. Idle and unutilised land and violent conflicts are evidence of such costs and of limitations to the success of patronage in regulating access to land.

Case 2: Struggles over Public 'but' Private Land

Victims of the first and second waves of eviction that accompanied the expansion of the plantation expected to get back the land upon expiry of the lease. In about 1992 the lease on one block expired but it did not revert back to those who had been evicted. It allegedly reverted back to government ownership. No sooner had this happened than the lease was renewed and part subleased to a cement company. The plantation retained the other part. The company constructed a brick perimeter fence around the disputed land in an effort to fence off the squatters. Both events put a lid on the rising expectations of resettlement. To regain the land, some of the area's residents approached two local Members of Parliament while others directed their appeals to the District Commissioner (DC) and the Provincial Commissioner (PC). All these appeals were said to have been unsuccessful. The politicians simply said the matter would be resolved by the Provincial Administration while the latter asked the squatters to 'keep peace as the government inquired into the matter'. All those consulted apparently skirted the issue partly because more powerful actors had been involved in the lease negotiations and partly because they feared a political backlash. In addition to this, both the cement company and the plantation owners had maintained relations with central state elites over a long period of time as a way of keeping the state away from the land question in the area. As informants observed, 'the plantation's principal shareholders had institutionalised the practice of buying off local politicians after every general election'. This practice had extended to cover maverick local elites. But since some of the local-level leaders were squatters or had no secure tenure on their land, it was difficult to develop a comprehensive patronage approach and specifically one that would have 'silenced' all the 'land-needy' elites.

A political differentiation between the district's national and local-level elites was clearly evident in relation to the issue of patronage. Their positions and the way in which they related to the land question brought them riches and connected them to the powerful. This tended to deter them from involvement in actual struggles over land; they often blamed and sought solutions through the administrative context, while side stepping the issue of 'land grabbing' by national level political and influential economic elites.

There were also local level elites who commanded considerable local support because of consistently articulating local land issues. In their ranks were several local state party officials – including a councillor, members of the opposition political parties, a local cleric, a school teacher, and a local women's group leader. Their approach was distinct from that of national level elected officials in several ways. This group mobilised resistance against land grabbing and articulated the problem against both the administrative and political contexts. The local level elites acted as a link between the mass of the squatters and the elected officials and the Provincial Administration. They were de facto leaders of the opposition to 'irregular allocations' and had constituted a 'squatters committee'. This committee articulated popular concerns on squatting and kept abreast with all aspects of the land question.

From late 1995, it was this group of local level elites who mobilised the squatters into occupying the section of the plantation whose lease had expired with a view to redistributing the land among the squatters. By early 1996 they had devised a plan for redistribution: they listed the names of the rightful occupants and made several attempts to discuss the subleased land with the DC and the PC but nobody was willing to meet them until they heard about the plans to subdivide the land.

In February 1996, the PC conceded to a meeting in which the squatters committee enumerated the problems the squatters wanted a solution to. The committee emphasised that their land continues to be grabbed by 'deceitful outsiders' while a lot more was 'expropriated for plantation farming'. They stressed that 'squatting had become a chronic wound stuck on us from the days of our forefathers'. They wondered 'how come a stranger (foreigners and/or upcountry elites) owns our property while we are made slaves in our ancestral land?' The PC only promised to 'soon look into the problems' and assured them that the Presidential directives on the resettlement of squatters and adjudication of rights on the land they occupied would be effected. Afraid that the promise would turn into an empty one like the previous ones, the squatters organised to 'invade' the farm and subdivide it. The land 'redistribution project', unlike the one in the formal resettlement schemes, was organised through a committee appointed by the occupants. The committee comprised elders, the youth, and the local level leaders. This committee helped identify genuine inhabitants and listed their names. The youth watched out for intruders and possible attacks by the police. The local leaders continued to consult with the Provincial Administration at different levels.

The redistribution project began by uprooting the sisal, subdividing the holdings and allocating them to those listed and participating in the project. As the exercise went on, the plantation owners called for the intervention of the DC who came in the company of the police. The DC did not manage to stop the redistribution partly because of the hostility of the squatters and partly because of continuing consultations between the PC and the local level elites. The PC held a meeting and, in response to their complaints, announced the setting aside of more land for the resettlement of squatters but this was seen as inadequate for the high number of landless registered by the squatters committee.

The struggle did not come to an end with the setting aside of the land: the plantation owners insisted that they would not transfer any more land unless they got title to another block whose lease had expired and had been reconverted into government land. Whether they really succeeded in having the allocations revoked is debatable but cannot be ruled out, given that the plantation owners had over the years sharpened their 'political skills' to deal with the political and administrative contexts of the land question in the area.

The above discussion raises several points. First, patronage deepened rather than solved the squatter problem because 'grants from above' reduced the size of land meant for resettlement. There was more concentration of land by political and economic elites and consequent dispossession of the squatters. Patronage as a means of accessing land rights became so institutionalised that even some of the squatters depended on it to secure their rights. Second, counter-patronage strategies or popular modes of acquiring land rights evolved when patronage failed or where patronage hierarchies were weak and unable to deliver. It is precisely because patronage failed to yield that the squatters invaded the sisal plantation and redistributed land amongst themselves. Both the landless and squatters also could not effectively utilise the holdings they squatted on because of the ever-present threat of eviction, a threat they considered a 'chronic wound' in their daily struggles. On the other hand, those allocated land 'from above' were speculating and not using it: they planned to erect hotels or to sell to hoteliers. Few used it for agriculture as the squatters did. These allocations therefore should be seen as involving conflict over access as well as conflict over land use. Finally, the discussion shows that patronage has its costs for the elites as well. It generated disputes between them as it did between themselves and squatters and therefore it is not a 'problem-free' mode of acquiring rights or building political constituencies.

Case 3: The Politics of Land Tenure Reform in Coastal Kenya

The land reform programme in Coastal Kenya began in the period between the late 1960s and early 1970s. Studies have demonstrated how the reform led to some people losing or gaining more rights to land. Others have attempted to assess the impact of the reform on the society in general [*Mkangi, 1975; Fleuret 1988; Ciekawy, 1988*]. How the reform programme affected community and wider politics has nonetheless received scant attention. Although the reform began in the late 1960s not much land has been adjudicated or registered: few people have title deeds. The reasons for this include disputes among the local people over the different stages of the reform and in particular the demarcation stage which delineates people's rights before they are registered.

Another problem has been the lack of adequate resources on the part of the government to support the reform. When such resources are available they are spent in demarcating land along the coastal line where influential political elites have an interest in beach plots for the rapidly growing tourist industry. This notwithstanding, political impulses have considerably speeded up the exercise since the mid-1980s. This is particularly true with regard to demarcation of squatters' rights in government land. In Kilifi district, between early mid-1980 and 1995, 40 blocks of government land in different places and covering an area of over 12,920 hectares were adjudicated to over 14,040 squatters already settled there. In total only about 20 per cent of the land has been registered since the early 1970s. Presidential directives considerably influenced the pace of the demarcation and adjudication of land here. Government officers often got into action whenever the president issued directives to speed up the exercise but thereafter the pace slowed down.

Where land registration was going on, most disputes centred around boundaries and ownership of land. Some disputes were occasioned by disagreements between and among family members; others resulted from people reneging on previous agreements on the rights allowed; yet others resulted from instances where parents died without clarifying to their children the kind of rights they had, especially important given that the indigenous tenure allowed for the coexistence of tree and land rights in the same holding. Disputes were common in instances where pioneer occupants acquired land to cultivate or to grow tree crops but lent out some sections or fragments to other families or even allowed borrowers to cultivate food crops under their trees on the understanding that the 'borrowers acknowledged having nothing more than user rights'.

Arbitrators in some of these disputes were village elders who were assumed to have the knowledge of 'which family used to own what and where'. They heard these disputes in the presence of both the local chief and the adjudication officers. If they were unable to resolve it then they advised the disputants to take their dispute to the local land Adjudication Committee who would hear it and advise the adjudication officer on how to proceed with the registration of disputed rights. If still dissatisfied, the disputants would proceed to the Land Arbitration Board, a body comprising between six and twenty five residents from within the district and appointed by the Provincial Commissioner. Most members of the Board were retired government officers, elders, and other prominent people 'who are likely to avoid bribes'. This Board heard cases from all over the district but met quite irregularly. Cases brought to the Board took slightly longer than those heard by the local land Adjudication Committee. Once the adjudication register was published those still dissatisfied with the Arbitration Board could make an appeal to the Minister of Lands. But cases brought to both the Arbitration Board and Minister took a long time to determine and involved costs that ordinary disputants were not able to bear.

All cases of dissatisfaction were referred from the lower legal authority to a higher one. Some were resolved by informal negotiations outside of the arbitration of the authorities while other disputants preferred to appeal to higher levels of the Provincial Administration. This was generally practised by those who lost cases at the level of the Adjudication Committee. Moreover, whether to go to the local Provincial Administration or any other authorities depended on various considerations. Some chose to go to the chiefs or District Officers if their rivals had already gone to the Committee. For others the choice was influenced by the costs involved in filing a case. Attempts were always made by each arbitrating body to ensure that all disputants were present when the case was being heard. Both the District Officers (DOs) and the adjudication officers (for the Committee) often consulted to decide on who would hear any case brought to their attention because 'some were civil cases that had issues of land subordinated to them'.

The option of going to the courts was generally discouraged because of the Presidential directive that land disputes should not be heard by courts and because jurisdiction to determine land disputes per se had been transferred from the magistrate's law courts to the elders' courts chaired by District Officers. The 'modern' court's responsibilities are currently confined to giving the decisions of the elders' court's legal force by certifying the proceedings of the elders' courts. Family disputes over boundaries cooled down faster than those about actual ownerships and records of existing rights, that is, records of who owns how much and where. These were often the main subject of arbitration by the different bodies.

Most informants felt that the reform programme had progressed at a very slow pace. They identified several factors responsible for this. A majority observed that the reform was held up by delays in solving disputes over demarcation of boundaries and over 'records of existing rights'. The rich, officers in the Provincial Administration and Lands Office and corruption in general were also identified as impediments. Those who cited corruption specifically accused the Committee and the adjudication officers of settling disputes in favour of those who had bribed them. The rich, the influential and local elites in general, were perceived as instrumental in the registration because they had '*uwezo*' (the monetary means) to influence the Committee and the adjudication officers in their favour, irrespective of whether they had legitimate rights and claims. This had the effect of intensifying disputes over both boundaries and the 'records of existing rights' between such people and others who had legitimate claims but no '*uwezo* to sway the Committee or the land officers to their side'.

Although some of the respondents saw the adjudication staff as being vulnerable to elite manipulation, the local elites resented the staff in the Departments of Lands and Settlement, Survey, and the Physical Planning because 'they all come from upcountry and therefore have little regard for the pace of the programme'. These officers, on the other hand, gave other reasons for the slow pace of the reform programme. They claimed that the Department lacked both funds and personnel. They specifically cited transport difficulties, lack of field allowances, lack of equipment, and shortage of aerial and base maps as handicaps to their work. Pressing assignments were carried out with vehicles borrowed from other departments, and their use depended on the availability of funds for fuel. These constraints led to funds for many activities such as re-demarcating boundaries or subdividing holdings being solicited from those who came for such services. Those who were able to pay for transport got their problems attended to while those who were unable to pay had to wait for the Department to get funds from the parent ministry which in turn depended on the availability of funds from the Treasury.

The adjudication staff also blamed the slow progress on disputes among residents, arguing that disputes often degenerated into violent confrontations thereby making some areas inaccessible. They cited disputes involving families, clans, and adjudication of rights of occupants on government land as the main examples in this regard. Government land was said to be even more inaccessible because of disagreements among squatters about the boundaries of their rights. The status of Arab and Swahili land, whose owners had not registered their rights, also hindered the progress of the reform particularly where such lands bordered government land and/or were occupied by squatters. Since the policy required the presence of land owners in the adjudication processes for purposes of determining boundaries it was difficult to register any land that bordered on Arab and Swahili land in the absence of these landowners.

The reform programme was thus implemented under severe constraints.

The financial burden was slowly transferred to the community and particularly to those who sought land-related services. The restrictions on government spending on the land reforms meant that the local communities had to shoulder the increasing costs of the reform. Meanwhile, an informal 'rent seeking' mechanism developed which benefited land officers and wealthy residents. Generally control of land became a political resource for both 'low' and 'high' politics in addition to providing economic resources for mediating patronage based politics. One may conclude therefore that while both administrative fiat and political whims influenced the pace or the progress of the reform, they also largely contributed to the deepening of the land question and to the intensification of disputes in the area.

POLITICS OF LAND RIGHTS AND SOCIAL DOMINATION

The issue of land ownership has been at the centre stage of local politics in Kenya for a long while. With regard to the coast, land rights generated political conflicts similar to those experienced upcountry. In the run up to independence in 1963, differences between the Arabs and the Swahili and the Mijikenda groups led to socio-political divisions along which several political parties formed. After independence, the resettlement schemes caused sharp hostilities between upcountry groups and indigenous coastal ethnic groups. Concerns by the latter's political leaders, resulted in the appointment of a government committee to investigate and make recommendations on the land question. Recommendations received little attention. Government land was increasingly turned over to economic and political elites for the purposes of tourism which state elites seemed keen on promoting.

This situation obtained for a short period after Moi ascended to the Presidency in 1978 but was reinforced after his social bases of support began to decline. 'Grants from above' linked to short-term political considerations. Allocations were made with a view to concentrating power and securing loyalty from the elite rather than in accordance with broader economic or political objectives. This resulted in increased landlessness and a deepening of the squatter problem around the coast. These problems, in addition to the problems arising from the reform of land tenure, became the single most important resource for mobilising political support.

Although articulation of land issues plays a critical role in political mobilisation, those elected into office failed to continue to press for viable solutions to it. The central state elites and others in privileged political and economic positions 'silenced' them with grants of land or other favours so that they would not adopt positions which were detrimental to their modes of accumulation. In this way, the national political elites' role prevented the consolidation of an active constituency of landless.

Social and political divisions among the various coastal groups also contributed to the lack of a common and consistent position on the land question. Divisions between the heterogenous Mijikenda groups and especially between the Giriama, the Chonyi and the Kauma in Kilifi are reproduced in the organisation of area electoral politics. Rarely did these different groups assume a common position on land issues as each inhabited a distinct geographical location. Problems of one subgroup were rarely seen as universal problems but as localised to that specific group. Political elites contributed to the widening of this divide since it enabled them to have effective control over politics and the economy.

The reform of land tenure has been accompanied by different types of disputes, of which the main ones concern boundaries and ownership of holdings. Transformation of land into an important patronage resource also had adverse effects on the previous modes of accessing and controlling land. Most beneficiaries did not utilise the land but turned their 'grants from above' over to private developers. The implications of this for the national economy are very clear. First, at the national economic level, this mode of accumulation has eroded the basis of indigenous capitalism and replaced it with Asian and foreign capital, but with connections to central state elites. Second, at the local level, this form of accumulation has resulted in the economic and social domination of the local people. Third, economic structures created by these forms of accumulation are not responsive to local needs; they are associated with 'private forms of repression' which are channelled through local state structures – the Provincial Administration officers.

The state-led mode of social-economic domination and exclusion has bifurcated the society into a group of the landed, and therefore economically and politically powerful, and a group of squatters or 'subjects of the landlords' who are increasingly determined to solve the land question and to secure land rights. The local state structures continue to act as the main avenues through which this 'subjection' and social domination is enforced.

The involvement of the state in regulating access to public land has increased rather than decreased. The state has contributed to the deepening of the land question rather than solved it. The state's practice of individualising public land according to political considerations has created more people without rights to land and by that generated new types of disputes over ownership; it has re-configured the broad context through which the indigenous accessed land rights. The most important of these concerns 'allocations of public land' (done on prime high potential areas) which result in the mass eviction of those already settled and ride roughshod over the improvements they have made during their long period of occupancy.

Yet political patronage has its own 'expenses' and limitations: the success of 'accumulation from above' requires not only political connections (or even higher political connections) but a 'regime of compulsions' and/or administrative and legal force. 'Resistance from below', the single most important mechanism for limiting such forms of accumulation, also has its own internal contradictions and limitations. Social-economic and political differentiation among the actors involved prevents the consolidation of popular opposition against patronage both by institutions of the state at the local level and by private economic elites.

What has come to be known as the land question cannot be reduced to a single issue and solution. Its complexity and dynamism cannot be fully captured by defining it as a simple question of relations of agricultural productivity to titling. This discussion suggests that land tenure reform hinges not only on issues of land productivity but also on issues of social restructuring, polarisation and exclusion. In other words, the question of land rights has an important political dimension: the politically weak groups are less capable of gaining rights to land when faced with politically and economically powerful groups. Moreover, even where they are capable of gaining rights to land, they lack the mechanisms of enforcing and securing them. The 'land question complex' must, therefore, be understood as one constitutive of the social, political and economic relations in an agrarian social formation. Any meaningful attempt to resolve the political and economic crises around land rights must first appreciate this complexity.

REFERENCES

Basset, J.T. and Donald E. Crummey (eds.), 1993, *Land in African Agrarian Systems*, Madison, WI: University of Wisconsin Press.
Bates, R., 1989, *Beyond the Miracle of the Market: The Political Economy of Agrarian Development in Kenya*, Cambridge: Cambridge University Press.
Berry, S., 1993, *No Condition is Permanent: The Social Dynamics of Agrarian Change in Sub-Sahara Africa*, Madison, WI: University of Wisconsin Press.
Charo, J. B., 1977, 'The Impact of Land Adjudication under the Titles Act Cap. 282 in Kilifi District', LLB Dissertation, University of Nairobi.
Ciekawy, D., 1988, 'Land Reform in Kenya's Southern Kilifi District, 1955-87', *East African Research and Development*, Vol.18, pp.164–80.
Cooper, F., 1980, *From Slaves to Squatters: Plantation Labour and Agriculture in Zanzibar and Coastal Kenya, 1890–1925*, New Haven, CT: Yale University Press.
Fleuret, A., 1988, 'Some Consequences of Tenure and Agrarian Reform in Taita Taveta, Kenya', in R.E. Downs and S.P. Reyna (eds.), *Land and Society in Contemporary Africa*, London: University Press of New England.
Ghai, V.P and J.W.B. McAuslan, 1970, *Public Law and Political Change in Kenya*, Nairobi: Oxford University Press.
Glazier, J., 1985, *Land Use and Uses of Tradition among the Mbere of Kenya*, Lanham, MD: University Press of America.
Harbeson, J.W., 1973, *Nation Building in Kenya: The Role of Land Reform*, Evanston, IL: North-Western European Press.
Leo, C., 1985, *Land and Class in Kenya*, Harare: Nehands.
Leys, C., 1975, *Underdevelopment in Kenya: The Political Economy of Neo-colonialism 1964–1971*, Berkeley, CA: University of California Press.

Mamdani, M., 1996, *Citizen and Subject: Contemporary Africa and the Legacy of Late Colonialism*, Princeton, NJ: Princeton University Press.

Mkangi, G.C., 1975, 'Land Tenure, Population Growth, and Economic Differentiation: The Ribe Tribe of Kenya', in T.S. Epstein and D. Jackson (eds.), *The Paradox of Poverty*, New Delhi: Macmillan.

Njeru, E. H. N., 1978, 'Land Adjudication and its Implications for the Social Organization of the Mbere', Research Paper No.73, Madison, WI: University of Wisconsin-Madison, Land Tenure Centre.

Njonjo, A,. 1978, 'The Africanisation of the White Highlands: A Study in Agrarian Class Struggles in Kenya, 1950–1974', Ph.D. Dissertation, Princeton University.

Okoth-Ogendo, W.H.O., 1976, 'African Land Tenure Reform', in J. Heyer (ed.), *Agricultural Development in Kenya*, Nairobi: Oxford University Press.

Okoth-Ogendo, W.H.O., 1979, 'Imposition of Property Law in Kenya', in B. Harrell-Bond and S. Burman (eds.), *The Imposition of Law*, New York: Academic Press.

Okoth-Ogendo, W.H.O., 1987, 'The Perils of Land Reform: The Case of Kenya', in J. Arntzen, L. Ngcngco, and S. Turner (eds.), *Land Policy and Agriculture in Eastern and Southern Africa*, Tokyo: United Nations University Press.

Okoth-Ogendo, W.H.O., 1991, *Tenants of the Crown*, Nairobi: ACTS Press.

Platteau, J. ., 1996, 'The Evolutionary Theory of Land Rights As Applied to Sub-Saharan Africa: A Critical Assessment', *Development and Change*, Vol.27, pp.29–86.

Republic of Kenya, 1978, *Report of Parliamentary Select Committee on Landlessness along the Coast*, Nairobi: Government Printers.

Salim, A.I., 1968, 'The Movement for Mwambao or Coastal Autonomy in Kenya, 1956–63', in B.A. Ogot (ed.), *Hadith 2: Proceedings of the 1968 Conference of the Historical Association on Kenya*, Nairobi: East African Publishing House.

Sorrenson, M.P.K., 1967, *Land Reform in the Kikuyu Country: A Case in Government Policy*, Nairobi: Oxford University Press.

Sorrenson, M.P.K., 1968, *Origin of European Settlement in Kenya*, Nairobi: Oxford University Press.

Swynnerton, J.M., 1954, *A Plan to Intensify the Development of African Agriculture in Kenya, Colony and Protectorate of Kenya*, Nairobi: Government Printers.

World Bank, 1989, *Sub-Saharan Africa: From Crisis to Sustainable Growth*, Washington, DC: The World Bank.

Past Wrongs and Gender Rights: Issues and Conflicts in South Africa's Land Reform

SUSIE JACOBS

South Africa's agrarian situation presents a range of daunting issues, including extreme rural poverty and a government hindered by severe financial constraints. At the same time, the country's attempts to incorporate gender issues into land reform, are virtually unique. The study discusses several major issues which confront the present Pilot Programme, and any future reform: demand for land; demand for services; the issue of 'the household'; traditional authorities; forms of land tenure; and the nature of public participation. The analysis stresses that all of these are gender issues, as is the extent of conflict raised through overt discussion of gender processes. None of these questions has a straightforward 'answer' but their consideration is likely instead to raise additional questions.

The government of South Africa is commencing a programme of land restitution and reform: the 1994 Restitution of Land Rights Act was the first substantive statute enacted by the new Parliament. It is attempting to meet various groups' claims to land arising from the racialised dispossession of segregation and apartheid, and to redistribute additional land in order to alleviate massive rural poverty. In its policy and programmes, the Department of Land Affairs (DLA) – responsible for land reform – also seeks to adhere to the 1996 constitutional provision concerning gender equity. The question of gender is particularly fraught in regard to land rights/entitlements in largely patrilineal and male-dominated rural areas, and female claims to land often oppose – or are seen as opposed to – other types of claims. State policies run the risk of simply making programmatic statements unless gender concerns are

Susie Jacobs, Department of Sociology, Manchester Metropolitan University, Rosamund Street West, off Oxford Road, Manchester M15 6LL, UK. The author would like to acknowledge financial assistance from the British Academy to attend the International Conference on Land Tenure in the Developing World, held at the University of Cape Town in January 1998. Thanks too to Ben Cousins and Andries DuToit of the Programme for Land and Agrarian Studies, University of the Western Cape, and to Jackie Sunde (Centre for Rural Legal Studies) and Nombelelo Siqwana-Ndulo (University of the Transkei) for access to some unpublished papers to which reference is made.

taken very seriously. And viewing gender as a critical factor will entail a willingness and capacity to mediate the conflicts which will ensue and which are already occurring.

THE AGRARIAN SITUATION

South Africa's agrarian situation has been analysed as 'extreme and exceptional' [*Bernstein, 1996b*]. Under apartheid laws, African and Coloured people were pushed onto 13 per cent of the land in 'Reserves/bantustans', much of it barely arable in a context in which only 15 per cent of the country's land is fully so [*Marcus, Eales and Wildschut, 1996: 101*]. The majority of the country's population is classed as in poverty, and severe poverty and are concentrated in the three provinces where bantustans were located: Mpumalanga, the Eastern Cape and KwaZulu Natal [*Meer, 1997b*]. Massive and repeated dispossessions have taken place, so that the majority of rural people do not live on their 'own' (ancestral) land; many have been moved numerous times. Additionally, various forms of state tenure were imposed.[1] Not surprisingly, there is much chaos concerning land claims and rights [*Cross and Rutsch, 1995*]. South Africa is also unusual in the context of international land reforms in that much of the population is already urbanised: in 1994, 65 per cent of all South Africans were 'functionally urbanised', including (an estimate of) 56 per cent of all bantustan residents [*Bernstein, 1996b: 29*]. Due to a variety of factors including neglect, 'betterment' planning, lack of opportunities for black smallholders, lack of viability of land, the dominance of the industrial economy and the great violence of the apartheid years, agriculture is no longer a main activity in the ex-bantustans [*Cross, 1988*]. Remittances form a major source of income [*Cobbett, 1988; Marcus, Eales and Wildschut, 1996*] and most people rely on a variety of activities to survive.

Thus 'agriculture' is often taken to mean large-scale farms, since agricultural output and employment is dominated by (mainly) white-owned estates numbering approximately 55,000 [*Levin, 1996: 54*]. These have been favoured with massive state subsidies for many years and farmers have a strong political and organisational forum in the South African Agricultural Union. Michael Lipton [*1996: 2*] points out that South Africa has been artificially 'deagriculturalised': farming provides fewer livelihoods than is generally associated with the country's overall level of development. Nevertheless, farm work looms large in the livelihoods of many.

This study focuses on gender concerns in South Africa's land reform. Before discussing such concerns in more detail, I contextualise. The next section examines the experience of gender and land reforms internationally and outlines some general debates concerning the country's land reform and the current legislation.

LAND REFORM AND GENDER INTERNATIONALLY

Within South African debates, gender issues are assuming more prominence. That gender issues are elaborated at all within current policy formation – whatever the limitations – should be seen as another feature marking South Africa as 'exceptional'. Little is known, seemingly, about gender and land reforms internationally; this may be because gender is usually 'written out' of standard – even 'progressive' or left – accounts of land reform. What is known, appears to be ignored.

When seen through a gendered lens, the experience of gender relations and women's rights within land reforms have not been happy. This is particularly so when seen from the perspective of (most) married women. With land reforms along individual family lines (as opposed to more collectivist strategies) land is usually allotted to 'household heads' who are nearly always seen as the husband/father, though sometimes with the inclusion of widows/deserted women with dependents. This structural factor sets a framework of inequity, although within this – and no doubt due in part to rural women's own agency – benefits do occur.

The similarity of effects of land reform for women worldwide, despite very varying cultural contexts, is notable. Some of the aggregate effects for women are summarised below. Generalisations are based on a summary of 22 case studies in Africa, Asia and Latin America [Jacobs, 1997].

Some effects of land reform are beneficial. First, household incomes for those fortunate enough to take part in what are often limited reforms, often rise. One of the main aims of land reforms is to increase food security; this often occurs, and is crucial for all. For some women, the importance of this aspect outweighs all others. Other changes which women may report as 'positive' concern transformations of family structure, usually so that extended families are more geographically distant and so have less control. Particularly when, as in the majority of cases, such families are patrilineal and patrilocal, many younger wives welcome this change to a smaller and/or more nuclear family. In a few cases (among them, in Zimbabwe), wives report increased income under their own control [Jacobs, 1992; 1998].

Other changes are perceived as more 'negative' for (many) women. Wives may be under pressure to intensify their work to increase production, and to bear more children in order to supply labour for a larger plot. The workloads of many rural women may already be injurious to health, with a 15- or 16-hour day not being uncommon. The material benefits of individual family reforms may have to be 'exchanged' for some loss of autonomy. Studies worldwide report increased male control for a variety of reasons, the most straightforward of which is the continuous presence of the man. Additionally, married women may lose customary rights to the small amounts of land they control, as in parts of Africa and Southeast Asia. It is common for husbands to be defined as 'farmers' and for wives to be defined/redefined as 'housewives'. Where use of relatively 'advanced' technology is part of the reform, men usually dominate this, so that women's skills may decline in status. Hence any freedom gained from control by in-laws may be traded for an increase in control by the husband.

SOME CURRENT DEBATES

The factors outlined earlier – severe poverty, dispossession and the dominance of large-scale agriculture – form a backdrop to debates in South Africa over what type of land reform should occur. As Levin and Weiner have pointed out in various writings [*Levin, 1996; Levin and Weiner, 1996; 1997; Merle Lipton, 1996*], the ANC's rural organisation was never strong, and rural strategy has remained little developed until recently. In the past, the main focus of organisation was the urban townships, and many assumed that an agricultural collectivisation might take place and 'solve' agrarian questions. However, the 1994 settlement entailed a market-led strategy and in this context policy had to be quickly formulated.

Against the background outlined above, several major issues face any state strategy of land reform. Chief among these are the extent of reform; the extent of state involvement versus 'the market'; the social composition of the beneficiaries; issues of productivity; types of land tenure and the issue of gender equity.

Some policy-makers and academics favour only a limited reform: the ANC-affiliated Macro-Economic Research Group (MERG) recommended only a limited redistribution, mainly to benefit adult female cultivators [*Bernstein, 1996b: 32*]. Others [*Marcus, Eales and Wildschut, 1996*] caution against assumptions that small agriculture can be a 'motor of development', and against widespread redistribution [*Manona, 1998*]. More recently, pressures for a more extended land reform as part of a development strategy have accelerated – from those invading land, from academics, from NGOs and from policy-makers. Michael and Merle Lipton argue strongly for a national strategy based on small farming [*Lipton, de Klerk and Lipton, 1996*]. Others too call for widespread agrarian reform, although with less fixed belief in the 'small farming route' [*Bernstein, 1997; Cousins, 1997; Hargreaves, 1996a; Levin and Weiner, 1997*].

Thus at least two general scenarios for land reform are evident. The first strategy involves the continuation of the status quo, with the admission of a group of black farmers, and possibly the redistribution of some land to the poorest, possibly including women. (In this strategy, the redistributed land runs risks of becoming a 'dump'.) The World Bank commissioned several early studies of land reform and was heavily involved in preliminary planning [*Williams, 1996; LAPC, 1994*]. Since, then, however, it appears to have partially retreated in the face of local opposition (Hanekom, cited in Palmer, [*1996*]). Not surprisingly, the Bank wished/es for any reform to be market-led and to emphasise individual freehold tenure. Proposals favour encouragement of a class of 'yeoman' or 'emergent' farmers; they give preference to those who would use land in a 'productive' manner, that is, for commercial purposes [*Williams, 1996*].

Such recommendations are echoed in a 1996 book [*van Zyl and Binswanger, 1996*], whose authors have written for the organisation. These are for owner-operated enterprises which are *competitive family farms*; diminution in the size of most commercial farms; the role of government to be to ensure a 'level playing field'; broadened access to agricultural services; support and servicing mainly by the private sector, and increased reliance on markets, privatisation and decentralisation [*van Zyl, 1996: 603*]. In his summary, van Zyl writes approvingly of the measures to increase access to land for the poor (through restitution and land reform); however, a more pivotal role is allotted to increased access to land for small and medium commercial farmers [*van Zyl, 1996: 604*]. Elsewhere, warning is given of the Zimbabwean example: it is seen as distributing too much land, and to farmers too poor to cultivate efficiently [*Masilela and Weiner, 1996*]. Cross [*1998: 109*] implies that a 'back-door' route to the large-farm strategy is emerging in current debates (for instance, those at a Rural Livelihoods Conference, January, 1998) over the definition of 'small': in some quarters, 'small' farms are being envisaged not as one to five hectares in size but as between 50 to 200.

Political positions have gender implications, although they often remain subtextual. This strategy ignores that no 'level playing field' exists for the majority of women, who are the majority of the poor. At one point Christiansen does note that the poorest might be best served through strategies other than land reform: e.g. the informal sector, welfare, or waged work (but no mention is made of where the latter might be found) [*Christiansen, 1996: 385*].

The second strategy entails widening the agricultural base to allow for very small-scale and non-commercial producers; such a strategy would logically entail redistribution of larger amounts of land. Potentially, such a strategy could encompass a number of female producers. However, widening the agricultural base will meet financial constraints, given the 'willing-buyer/willing-seller' terms of the settlement, and given that the DLA's budget constituted 0.3 per cent of national expenditure in 1996/97 [*Meer, 1997: 137*].

Although I do not take up such issues here, it is important to note that assumptions concerning productivity form another, often unspoken, current in debates. It is often assumed that South African black farmers are herders, incapable of being good farmers [*Bernstein, 1996b: 36*] or simply that large agriculture is best, or that redistribution is too risky to attempt. Hall [1998] points out that in official policy, assumptions of 'equity' and efficiency/productivity are often assumed to run counter to one another, particularly with reference to gender issues [Pankhurst and Jacobs, 1988]. The Liptons' Chayanovian model, on the other hand, assumes that small farms will usually be more productive because of the intensified use of 'family' labour. In South Africa even more than elsewhere, 'family' labour refers in the main to that of married women, who are already overburdened with work.

Various studies indicate that there does exist demand for land among the rural population [Cousins, 1996; Cross, 1998; Levin and Weiner, 1997; Marcus, Eales and Wildschut, 1996; Murray, 1996], at least in the absence of industry being able to absorb all available labour. A Land and Agriculture Policy Centre (LAPC) survey of 2,000 respondents found that total demand for land would amount to 24 per cent of all land in South Africa (assuming that 67 per cent of those wishing for land actually lodged claims) [Marcus, Eales and Wildschut, 1996: 18]. For this reason, too, land reform and restitution are on the 'agenda' as central issues.

CURRENT LEGISLATION AND THE STATE OF LAND REFORM

That gender concerns are being seen as significant land reform policy issues is highly unusual. South Africa's policy formulation is due to the ANC's recognition of the importance of gender as a source of oppression [Seidman, 1993]; to pressure from South African women's organisations [Kemp et al., 1995] and to many policy-makers' recognition that gender is, at a minimum, an issue that should be incorporated.

Several measures have been enacted since 1994 in the arena of land rights. The government's programme deals with three aspects: restitution, tenure reform and redistribution. The 1994 Restitution of Land Rights Act (1994) has been noted. The Interim Protection of Informal Land Rights Act (1996) is a holding mechanism to protect existing informal rights until a longer-term measure is put in place. The Communal Property Associations Act (1996) makes it possible for groups to acquire land through the land reform programme in a communal property association, through which they can hold land. The latter must comply with constitutional principles of accountability, equity and democracy. The Land Reform (Labour Tenants) Act (1996) attempts to provide security to vulnerable labour tenants; the Extension of Security of Tenure Act (1997) prevents unfair evictions. Currently (February, 1998) legislation is being drafted to secure rights for people on the 13 per cent of 'bantustan' land [Budlender, 1998].[2]

Current land policy entails a commitment to gender equity, expressed in both the 1996 Green Paper of the DLA [1996] and the 1997 White Paper. Hall notes that gender equity is discussed in several sections of the latter document: for example, elimination of discrimination in women's access to land; gender equity in tenure reform (among others). However, mention of gender is entirely omitted in other, crucial sections, or else is mentioned only in passing. Such sections include: 'Land Development and Institutional Arrangements', Land Restitution Programmes and (crucially) Economic Arguments for Land Reform [Hall, 1998; DLA, 1997]. Most tellingly, women are treated as an 'add-on' category, as in the statement that the programme will assist 'labour tenants, farm workers, women as well as emergent farmers'. Thus, most beneficiary groups appear ungendered while 'women' appear to be without occupation [Hall, 1998: 223]. Such allusions appear frequently and also perpetuate the idea of women as classless. This is decidedly not the case, and women's class positions are likely to become increasingly differentiated. Land reform policies, while usually alleviating poverty [El-Ghonemy, 1990] also tend to promote class differentiation, affecting women as well as men, although in somewhat different ways [Jacobs, 1989].

Mention of women in this form tends to indicate ambivalence concerning how to incorporate 'women's' needs and interests. Such wording tends to veer away from examination of *gender* relations [Mathye, 1997], which would involve a more fundamental examination and rethinking than do 'add-on' categories.

At present, the land reform programme consists primarily of Pilot Programmes in the nine (new) provinces. Restitution claims are also proceeding, although in a piecemeal fashion. In 1996 Cloete and Naidoo [1996: 4] reported that the programme was progressing slowly, due in part to the 'willing-buyer/willing-seller' proviso. Although the original aim was to transfer 30 per cent of white-owned land to black smallholders (a World Bank figure) [Williams, 1996], this has been scaled down to provision of cash grants of Rand 15,000 (about £2,000) to selected rural households. In early 1998, Cross reports that delivery of land transfers is speeding up, with many land transfers in the pipeline [Cross, 1998: 101]. She further warns that at present rural economic systems are in disarray, and edging towards collapse, with much uncertainty over tenure rights, and outbreaks of 'land-grabbing' [Cross, 1997]. Many writers point to a lack of capacity of underfunded local and national states to deliver and to provide back-up in forms such as services and adjudication [Cousins, 1997; Bernstein, 1997; Cocks and Kinsgwill, 1998; Cross, 1997; 1998; Levin and Weiner, 1997].[3]

GENDER ISSUES IN SOUTH AFRICA'S LAND REFORM

The general context of South African land reform is, then, exceedingly complex.[4] Such complexity is compounded by gender. Under 'national democratic transformation', as Levin [*1996: 53*] points out, conditions exist for facilitating access to land without gender discrimination. However, despite the commitment to gender equity expressed in the Green and White Papers, practices, structures and discourses which seriously disadvantage most rural black women continue.

In the following, I discuss seven major gender issues. This is, of course, not an exhaustive list, since most phenomena have gender dimensions.

Demand for Land

A first issue is the demand for land, of significance in a 'demand-led' policy [*Hall, 1998*]. The Land and Agriculture Policy Centre's (LAPC) survey indicated that the main demand for land in the country is for residential purposes, reflecting widespread homelessness post-apartheid [*Marcus et al., 1996*]. People, and particularly women, expect or hope for provision of basic services such as water, schools, shops and clinics [*Cocks and Kingswill, 1998*], although at the moment government is often unable to meet such demand. Men often wished for land for grazing stock; both sexes expressed the need for land to cultivate. However, those with land – mainly though not exclusively men – desired/expected far more than, on average, than those without – mainly women. Marcus, Eales and Wildschut [*1996: 16-17*] found that men expressed a need for on average six times the amount of land women desired or felt empowered to say they wanted. Cross [*1998: 11*] writes that men were usually unwilling to cultivate less than two hectares, while women were willing to 'make do' on fewer resources. The pattern which emerges from these findings is that most men desire land for commercial cultivation and grazing, while most women opt for a multi-livelihood strategy based around food security.

Further points should be made. The LAPC survey also found that class factors were of significance in the desire for land. Questions of identity, too, were of import: men are far more likely to be seen and to see themselves as 'farmers'. It is conceivable that in future women – or perhaps only better off women – might expect land for commercial purposes. Identity being malleable, they may also identify as potential farmers.

Demand for Services

A second issue concerns the importance of provision of support and of services as well as land. Women are the great majority of permanent rural dwellers; one Transkei study (Bembridge [*1988*], cited in Meer (ed.) [*1997: 141*]) found 71 per cent of adult women to be managing farms on their own. Most of the poor, men and women, lack access to basic amenities such as clean water, toilets and clinics. Middleton's [*1997: 80*] case study on the ex-Ciskei-Transkei border found that women wished for residential and garden land, but also for clinics, creches, shops, water, toilets and electricity. At present the DLA's remit stops at land redistribution, with no plans (or budget) for wider strategies [*Meer (ed.)*, *1997*]. A land reform which will benefit the majority of women would require provision of services as well as acquisition of land [*Jacobs, 1992*], particularly in a situation where many households have used up scant savings to acquire land. Importantly, rural women in South Africa as elsewhere require access to credit [*Mathye, 1997; Pankhurst and Jacobs, 1988*] as well as to agricultural extension services. Their (usual) lack of ability to command labour is an additional quandary – one even more difficult to rectify than lack of credit.

'The Household'

A third issue concerns the continued use of the 'household' as the unit of subsidy within the Pilot Land Reform programmes. Registration for the subsidy is in the name of adult beneficiary members, not simply the head of household. Although in an international context this constitutes a 'gender-aware' step, problems remain. As a large body of feminist work has established, households- or many households – are not undifferentiated entities with equal internal redistribution [*Folbre, 1988*]. The Transvaal Rural Action Committee (TRAC) has expressed concern that the most vulnerable with households will not benefit from the subsidy. Additionally, it suggests that the subsidy be extended to cover the gendered needs outlined above, as well as creches [*Hargreaves, 1996b: 5*]. Reports are emerging of married women's and single women's difficulties in accessing land. Despite their formal entitlement, married women and most single women are not seen as socially entitled to hold land, given customary law and expectations and household gender power relations [*Sunde and Hamman, 1996: 27; Siqwana-Ndulo, 1996*]. Most studies agree that rural women across South Africa have few decision-making powers independent of husbands [*Cross and Friedman, 1997; Levin, 1996; Marcus et al., 1996; Meer, 1997a; Siqwana-Ndulo, 1996; Sunde and Hamman, 1996*], even in men's absence through migration. Although a 1993 law removed the concept of 'marital power', marriages contracted under customary law (that is, the majority of rural marriages) are exempted [*Fagan, et al., 1996*].[5]

Several studies indicate that male domination often extends to the authority of adult sons over mothers. For although the law in KwaZulu-Natal since 1987 has allowed female household heads to acquire land in their own right, few do so; most women who do, are inheriting widows [*Marcus, Eales and Wildschut, 1996: 91; Manona, 1998: 407*]. Cross and Friedman [*1997*] point out that women inheriting land often have it taken by husband's relatives, who stake a claim. Siqwana-Ndulo found, in an Eastern Cape (formerly, Transkei) sample, that not only did wives take *no* major decisions without consulting their husbands, widows took no major decisions without consulting eldest sons [*Siqwana-Ndulo, 1996: 5*]. Walker [*1997: 66*], too, notes ambiguities concerning widow-son authority relations and Small [*1997: 47*] writes of cases in which sons evict mothers upon disagreement. The core assumption underpinning widows' land rights and such conflicts in rural South Africa is that land will remain within the patrilineage, widows' landholding is legitimised, where it exists, because it is seen to be temporary. Only *never-married* women were free of such restrictions.

'Custom and tradition', then, continue to structure the lives and the land rights of rural and many urban women. (See Meer (ed.) [*1997*] for case studies.) Note that the terms 'custom' or 'tradition' should be accepted uncritically, in any context [*Hobsbawm and Ranger, 1984*]. What is today known as custom and tradition is in fact a product of a complex and dynamic history of contestation, cooption and reconstruction [*Walker, 1996*].

Traditional Authorities

A fourth and closely related issue is that of the authority of tribal/traditional leaders, who administer land rights in many ex-bantustan areas. Such authority, whether or not it reflects pre-capitalist 'custom', is and is likely to continue to be a difficult and contentious issue, for the establishment of local democracy, for more democratic gender relations and for any land reform. The MDM (Mass Democratic Movement) did make a start towards rural mobilisation [*Levin and Weiner, 1996*] and the ANC is currently gaining organisational strength [*Fife, 1996*]. Overall, however, few alternative structures exist to counter the power of traditional authorities.

Traditional leaders are often accused of corruption, patronage- mongering and brutality [*Marcus et al., 1996: 82 and 83; Levin and Weiner, 1996*] and of abuse of their roles in allocating land [*Eveleth, 1996: VI*]. There is evidence that they wish to extend, not simply to maintain, their areas of authority. Problems seem to arise particularly when leaders begin to draw power from political party rather than local community sources. This undermines local accountability and often leads chiefs to coercive and violent strategies [*McIntosh et al., 1996*].

However, chiefly authority also has positive features, and (despite the above remarks) retains legitimacy in many areas [*McIntosh et al., 1996*]. Cross [*1992*] details how informal and more egalitarian tenures emerge even at times under autocratic chiefly control. The 'African land ethic' stresses universal access to land and to other factors of subsistence, priority of use so that families with more land than they can use should transfer it to the land-hungry, continual exchange relations and transfer of occupancy, as well as the continuity of household or descent group access and seniority, granted to the first descent groups settling in an area. Marcus, Eales and Wildschut also note that the commitment of many chiefs to traditional tenure does arise from genuine concern with welfare and equity on the basis of group membership, usually, through kinship. If actual practices are often affected by corruption and patronage, then popular pressure to allocate land means that traditional authorities must pay some attention to the needs of the poorest and least powerful [*Marcus et al., 1996: 81–2*]. Thus absolute landlessness is less common in the highly-congested former reserves than on white-owned commercial farms.

Some developments are encouraging for prospects of gender equity. In one study, Mbatha and Albertyn [*1997*] found that in two NorthWest Provincial communities 'ANC-friendly' chiefs are partially abiding by official directives, in allocating land to married women as well as men. However, single women with children remain excluded at present.

While positive aspects of chiefly-administered tenures should be recognised, the power of traditional authorities, even tempered by an African land ethic, presents complexities and ambiguities for women. In Walker's [*1994; 1996*] analyses, chiefly authority is a serious problem. The ANC has tried to balance the interest of women's groupings and of traditional leaders, incorporating them both without recognising the contradictions. However, the influence of chiefs has been diminished in the new Constitution.

The above development is important. However, continued chiefly authority is unlikely to benefit women in most cases. Siqwana-Ndulo notes that chiefs at a workshop on land held at the University of the Transkei met the proposal that women be granted land with incredulity [*Siqwana-Ndulo, 1996: 6–7*], but she notes further that it is unlikely that new land reform areas can be administered without the assistance of such chiefs. And at a National Community Land Conference held in 1993, women's organisations made far-sighted demands for the abolition of polygyny and of the levirate, realising that the operation of landholding is intimately linked with kinship and descent systems. These motions were defeated, with traditional leaders being particularly opposed [*Walker, 1994*].

Land Tenure

A fifth (and interrelated) issue concerns type of land tenure. The advancement of women's land rights is often seen as synonymous with individual freehold tenure, and this may benefit some women. For instance, corporate outgrower schemes in KwaZulu Natal have benefited some women, nearly all widows, free of the need for husbands' permission [*Marcus et al., 1996*]. But the majority of rural women are unlikely to gain from unleashed market mechanisms. Moving from mediated to direct (that is, individually-allocated) land rights might leave many women with less land than they have access to at present. Thus a strong argument against women's entitlements being fixed to the idea of privatised, inalienable individual rights exists. In the 'large farm' strategy discussed above, 'people who would use the land productively' are likely to be, in the main, men. Few rural women would be in a position to take advantage of any opportunities market-driven reform might offer: they lack capital, recognised skills, education, and command over labour. For most women, prospects of regaining land through the market are slim.

Recognising these pitfalls, government has declared its intention of not titling land (or 'upgrading' it, as the misnomer goes) [*Budlender, 1998*] in the legislation now being formulated. The Communal Property Association Act 1996 also tries to avoid advantaging wealthier men through titling by allowing group-based membership of Communal Property Associations. These must have constitutions which provide for gender equality. This form is an innovative attempt to deal with the complexities of rural land tenure. Hopefully, future research will investigate whether this form is able to benefit poorer women.

Women and Public Participation

A sixth issue concerns women's relative lack of 'voice' in community-level structures and in decision-making. Policy-makers, NGOs and academics have begun to highlight this concern as one hindrance to an egalitarian land redistribution [*Cocks and Kingswill, 1998; Cross and Friedman, 1997; Fife, 1996; Hargreaves, 1996a; Mogale and Poshoko, 1997*]. Walker [*1997: 35*] notes that community decision-making structures are even more closed to most women than are household ones. Public fora are widely seen as 'male'; they are not envisaged as spaces in which women are empowered to speak – except, at times, for a handful of 'powerful' women [*DuToit, 1996*].

This point links with two others: women's general lack of social power, particularly where decision-making is overt rather than more hidden or covert; and the idea of 'community' itself. On-the-ground relationships involving close association – for example, kinship, neighbourhood, political association, friendship – do exist. However, the idea of 'community' in southern Africa as elsewhere, invokes 'imagined' unity while at times obscuring power relations. As noted above, in most South African rural areas, community power structures are dominated by older males and more generally decisions over land reflect men's land needs [*Marcus, Eales and Wildschut, 1996: 40*] – for example, for grazing, and for larger-scale production.

Pilot Land Reform Programmes incorporate a formal requirement that women participate in district and project planning [*Meer, 1997: 138*]. Hargreaves reports, however, that women's participation in the three areas for which evidence is available (the Western Cape, NorthWest Province, Mpumalanga) is not extensive [*Hargreaves, 1996a: 20*]. In Mpumlanga, four out of 15 members of the Management Committee, including the Chair, are female. This degree of inclusion of women probably reflects the strength in the area of the grassroots Rural Women's Movement [*Kemp et al., 1995*]. Even

82   DEVELOPMENT AND RIGHTS

where women are elected to committees, they may lack self-assurance
[*Hargreaves, 1996a: 22*]. Cloete and Naidoo [*1996: 6*] and DuToit [*1996*]
report that women attending meetings rarely voice their own opinions; the
former authors comment that they sometimes attend as the husband's delegate.
DuToit observes that through a variety of means, men often ensure that women
do not participate; some women collude in the process of 'silencing'. A more
general problem exists, of whether, and in what way, the physical presence of
women, even ones who do actively participate, translates into 'representation'
of gender issues [*Rai, 1996*].

Gender Power and Conflict?

The seventh point I raise refers not to a specific 'issue' but to underlying
processes. Land issues are deeply emotive. Land is linked to institutions and
processes such as family and kinship, community, gender roles and gender
power, and definitions of femininity and masculinity; changes within any or all
of these can be deeply disturbing. Several of the authors already cited begin to
touch upon such issues. Bernstein [*1996b: 38*] writes 'the most entrenched and
intractable of the "contradictions among the people" are gender relations'.
Meer [*1997: 34*] writes that broaching the subject of gender power relations
challenges deeply entrenched ways of knowing, theorising and doing.

Thus failures to confront or to prioritise gender issues is not simply a
failure of policy formulation, though it may be this as well. Or, to put the
matter another way: in order to formulate policies which will concretely
change the situation of rural women, especially the majority, the breadth and
depth of the 'question' must be openly considered.

It is not only one social category – that is, people acting in specific
roles/identities (for example, husbands) who may wish to inhibit changes in
gender (as well as class) relations. Meer (ed.) [*1997: 142*] mentions 'white
farmers, traditional authorities and men' as potentially threatened by
reorganisation of resource allocation. Male household heads and land
administrators are other 'threatened' categories [*Cross, 1998*]; sons as well as
some women may have interests in preserving most women's lack of power in
many spheres.

Cross and Friedman stand out in beginning to excavate the level of feeling
which underpins current debates and conflicts in the countryside. Many rural
men fear that if women gain land rights they will use their leverage to
overthrow the male-oriented system of power relations and familial social
order.

> Men often see themselves as managers of strategies which relate family
> to community ... [They] think that women will dispose of land rapidly
> and frivolously instead of using it judiciously for long-term political

goals. So men tend to see the suppression of women's attempts to hold and dispose of land, as an urgent *moral* (my emphasis) concern, part of their legitimate role in society ... change in gender control is seen [by many men] as linked with the destruction of rural society and of the family. Some women as well as men express such fears [*Cross and Friedman, 1997: 27–8*].

The sensation that things might materially and psychologically 'fall apart' is not an error of perception, or wholly an irrational fear, though fear it remains. It is an 'accurate' perception that men and women may use land differently, and that changes in relations on the land entail other widespread social changes, for instance in customary law; in women's visibility; in public power relations; in women's autonomy.

Perhaps not surprisingly, such defensiveness and anxieties are linked to the possibility of a backlash, at household, community and wider levels. Male violence is a common reaction to changes; even more common is the divorce and desertion sometimes noted as features of the region [*Cross and Friedman, 1997; Pankhurst and Jacobs, 1988*]. Mathye [*1997: 8*] points out that land tenure systems are sites of endemic violence, including violence towards women. She warns of some of the hazards of gender training, writing that this should not expose women to unnecessary risks.

Such gendered and sexualised conflicts are not specific to South Africa, but have occurred in many regions. While widespread conflicts do occur, it is not always the case that changes in gender relations are always conflictual. Walker notes for a KwaZulu-Natal study that rural household dynamics are undergoing change; nevertheless, most men and some women continue to adhere, at least verbally, to customary norms [*Walker, 1997: 70*].

And where conflicts become overt, this is not all negative. DuToit writes that it is true that gender issues are divisive and involve real possibilities of conflict. At the same time, addressing gender issues can access powerful constructive and healing energies within communities [*DuToit, 1996*]. Similarly, Arnfred [*1988: 11*], writing of 1980s Mozambique, comments that gender struggle is not (just) disruptive and destructive, but is also a means through which gender relations may change.

CONCLUSION

This study has noted that South African attempts to incorporate gender issues into an ongoing process of land reform, are virtually unique. This achievement should be recognised, while not impeding critique.

At the same time, the country's agrarian situation presents a range of daunting issues and problems, which people must live with, and which policy-makers must deal with: extreme rural poverty; dispossession; the power of traditional authorities; the chaotic situation in the countryside, and (relative) state incapacity, reinforced by financial constraints.

Gender lies at the heart of many of these questions. To recognise that they are, precisely, questions – they are open-ended and may have no clear solutions – may assist in considering them. Although it is likely that there exist 'better' and 'worse' approaches to reflecting upon and formulating policy about 'gender matters' (for example, recognising gender as pivotal instead of simply adding it in), integration of gender perspectives will tend to raise more questions rather than provide quick and easy solutions. The temporal aspect is of particular importance currently: the need to formulate perspectives and policies which will prioritise gender equity may conflict with rural people's pressing needs to acquire land to enhance their chances of food security and viable livelihoods [*Cocks and Kingswill, 1998*].

Widespread changes in gender relations and gender power are, moreover, unlikely to occur 'from above', although the power of states to influence and to facilitate movements should not be dismissed. Such changes, if they are to be long lasting, must come about from the grassroots. I do not wish to end in a stereotypically upbeat fashion, ignoring the possibility of reaction and backlash, or the risks of opposition and agency. At one level, however, changes are already occurring, through micro-processes of negotiation. This is the case even where public acknowledgement of shifts in gender roles is not made [*Walker, 1997*]. Women's confidence and their rural organisation is gaining strength in some areas, despite the constraints noted earlier. Women even in remote areas of KwaZulu Natal are beginning to speak out (Cross *et al.* [*1995*] cited in Cross and Friedman [*1997*]). Women in the Southern Cape Pilot Land Reform Project felt that they were living in 'historic times', which entailed, among other things, change in gender relations, including increased autonomy, respect and changes in the household division of labour [*DuToit, 1996*]. As Constance Mogale [*1997: 68*] of TRAC comments, '[the mothers feel that] it is time we make things feasible practically and not only verbally'. Many rural South African women are currently in struggle for such change.

NOTES

1. Forms of state tenure in South Africa include 'betterment' land planning (that is, forced villagisation with state-imposed conservation measures); trust tenure (in which land was bought by the South African Development Trust and which allowed the least control for black tenants); quitrent tenure (requiring a small annual rent in return for an independent lease and observation of approved farming techniques); state freehold, with restrictions on land use; state settlement schemes and state development leases [*Cross, 1992: 307*].
2. Geoff Budlender, the Director-General of the Department of Land Affairs stated that the new law being formulated will attempt to encompass reality 'on the ground'; that it would be rights and

not permit-based; that such rights would be vested in people not institutions, and that people will be able to choose the method of administering land.

3. As one example, Cousins [*1997*] notes that few in government know of the existence of the 1996 Interim Protection of Informal Land Rights Act.
4. To add further complexity, situations differ between regions and provinces. Such discussion, however, is beyond the scope of this article.
5. KwaZulu Natal Province is exempted from provisions of the 1993 Act, so that women can marry and remarry under the provision of 'marriage power' [*Fagan et al., 1996*].

REFERENCES

Arnfred, Signe, 1988, 'Women in Mozambique: Gender Struggle and Gender Politics', *Review of African Political Economy*, No.41.

Bembridge, T., 1988, 'The Role of Women in Agricultural and Rural Development in the Transkei', *Journal of Contemporary African Studies*, Vol.7, Nos.1–2.

Bernstein, Henry (ed.), 1996a, The Agrarian Question in South Africa, Special Issue of *The Journal of Peasant Studies,* Vol.23, Nos.2/3, pp.1–52.

Bernstein, Henry, 1996b, 'South Africa's Agrarian Question: Extreme and Exceptional?', in 'The Agrarian Question in South Africa', Special Issue of *The Journal of Peasant Studies,* Vol.23, Nos.2/3, pp.1–52.

Bernstein, Henry, 1997, 'Social Change in the South African Countryside: Land, Production, Property and Power', *Occasional Paper No.4*, Programme for Land and Agrarian Studies, University of the Western Cape.

Budlender, Geoff (Director-General, Department of Land Affairs), 1998, 'Opening Address', International Conference on Land Tenure in the Developing World, with Special Reference to southern Africa, University of Cape Town, 25–27 Jan.

Christiansen, R., 1996, 'An Overview of Land Reform Issues', in J. van Zyl and H. Binswanger, *Agricultural Land Reform in South Africa*, Oxford and Cape Town: Oxford University Press.

Cloete, Marian and Indran Naidoo, 1996, 'Land Reform Monitoring and Evaluation', Southern African Sociological Association Congress, Durban, July.

Cobbett, Matthew, 1988, 'The Land Question in a Post-Apartheid South Africa: A Preliminary Assessment', in Catherine Cross and Richard Haines (eds.), *Towards Freehold*, Cape Town: Juta, pp.60–72.

Cocks, Michelle and R. Kingswill, 1998, 'Land and Agrarian Reform: Transition and Continuity' in *Proceedings of the International Conference on Land Tenure in the Developing World*, University of Cape Town, January, pp.61–74.

Cousins, Ben, 1996, 'Livestock Production and Common Property Struggles in South Africa's Agrarian Reform', in The Agrarian Question in South Africa, Special Issue of *The Journal of Peasant Studies*, Vol.23, Nos.2/3, pp.166–208.

Cousins, Ben, 1997, 'How do Rights become Real?', *IDS Bulletin*, Vol.28, No.4, 5 Oct., pp.9–67.

Cross, Catherine, 1988, 'Freehold in the "Homelands": What are the Real Constraints?', in Cross and Haines (eds.), *Towards Freehold*, Cape Town: Juta, pp.337–77.

Cross, Catherine, 1992, 'An Alternate Legality: The Property Rights Question in Relation to South African Land Reform', *South African Journal on Human Rights*, pp.305–31.

Cross, Catherine, *et al.,* 1995, '"The Land is Not Enough": Land Reform District Study for KwaZulu Natal', LAPC, Johannesburg.

Cross, Catherine, 1997, 'Rural Land Tenure: Surrounded by Hungry Allocator', *Indicator SA*, Vol.14, No.2, pp.72–8.

Cross, Catherine, 1998, 'Reforming Land in South Africa: Who Owns the Land?', in *Proceedings of the International Conference on Land Tenure in the Developing World*, University of Cape Town, Jan., pp.101–16.

Cross, Catherine and Peter Rutsch, 1995, 'Losing the Land: Securing Tenure in Tribal Areas', *Indicator SA*, Vol.12, No.2, pp.23–8.

Cross, Catherine and Friedman, Michelle, 1997, 'Women and Land: Marginality and the Left Hand

Power', in S. Meer (ed.), *Women, Land and Authority*, Oxford: Oxfam, pp.17–34.

DLA, Department of Land Affairs, Republic of South Africa, 1996, *Our Land/Izwe Lethu*, Green Paper on South African Land Policy, Pretoria.

DLA, Department of Land Affairs, Republic of South Africa, 1997, *White Paper on South African Land Policy*, April, Pretoria.

DuToit, Andries, 1996, 'Problems in the Participation of Women in LRPP Community Structures in the Southern Cape', unpublished paper, Programme for Land and Agrarian Studies, Cape Town, University of the Western Cape.

El-Ghonemy, M. Riad, 1990, *The Political Economy of Rural Poverty: the Case for Land Reform*, London: Macmillan.

Eveleth, Ann, 1996, 'Battle for Local Democracy in KwaZulu has Just Begun', *Mail and Guardian Reconstruct Quarterly*, 12–18 July.

Fagan, G. Honor, Munck, R. and K. Nadasen, 1996, 'Gender, Culture and Development: A South African Cultural Perspective', in V. Tucker (ed.), *Cultural Perspectives on Development*, London and Portland, OR: Frank Cass.

Fife, Gordon, 1996, 'Local Government and Rural Livelihoods in the Western Cape', in Lipton, de Klerk and Lipton [*1996*].

Folbre, Nancy, 1988, 'The Black Four of Hearts: Towards a New Paradigm of Household Economics', in D. Dwyer and J. Bruce (eds.), *A Home Divided: Gender and Income in the Third World*, Stanford, CA: Stanford University Press.

Hall, Ruth, 1998, 'Design for Equity: Linking Objectives with Practice in Land Reform' in *Proceedings of the International Conference on Land Tenure in the Developing World*, University of Cape Town, Jan., pp.216–31.

Hargreaves, S., 1996a, 'Land Reform: Capturing Opportunities for Rural Women?', *Agenda*, No.30, pp.18–25.

Hargreaves, S., 1996b, 'The Land Reform Pilot Programme: Capturing Opportunities for Rural Women?', unpublished mimeo.

Hobsbawm, Eric and T.O. Ranger, (eds.), 1984, *The Invention of Tradition*, Cambridge: Cambridge University Press.

Jacobs, Susie, 1989, 'Gender Divisions and Land Resettlement in Zimbabwe', D.Phil thesis, Institute of Development Studies at the University of Sussex, Brighton.

Jacobs, Susie, 1992, 'Gender and Land Reform: Zimbabwe and Some Comparisons', *International Sociology*, Vol.7, No.1, pp.5–34.

Jacobs, Susie, 1997, 'Land to the Tiller? Gender Relations and Types of Land Reform', *Society in Transition*, Vol.21, Nos.1–4, pp.82–100.

Jacobs, Susie, 1998, 'The Gendered Politics of Land Reform: Three Comparative Studies', in V. Randall and G. Waylen (eds.) *Gender, Politics and the State*, Routledge: London.

Kemp, Amanda, Madlala, Nozizwe, Moodley, Asha and Elaine Salo, 1995, 'The Dawn of a New Day: Redefining South African Feminism', in A. Basu (ed.), *The Challenge of Local Feminisms*, Boulder, CO: Westview, pp.131–62.

LAPC (Land and Agricultural Policy Centre), 1994, 'Proceedings', Land Redistribution Options Conference, Johannesburg.

Levin, Richard, 1996, 'Land and Agrarian Questions in South Africa – A Socialist Perspective', *African Communist*, No.144, Second Quarter, pp.48–62.

Levin, Richard and Dan Weiner, 1996, 'The Politics of Land Reform in South Africa after Apartheid', in The Agrarian Question in South Africa, Special Issue of *The Journal of Peasant Studies*, Vol.23, Nos.2/3, pp.93–119.

Levin, Richard and Dan Weiner, 1997, *No More Tears: Struggles for Land in Mpumlanga, South Africa*, Trenton/Asmara: Africa World Press.

Lipton, Merle, 1996, 'The Politics of Rural Reform in South Africa' in Lipton, DeKlerk and Lipton [*1996, 401–37*].

Lipton, Michael, 1996, 'Rural Reforms and Rural Livelihoods: the Contexts of International Experience', in Lipton, deKlerk and Lipton [*1996*].

Lipton, Michael, deKlerk, Michael and Merle Lipton (eds.), 1996, *Land, Labour and Livelihoods in Rural South Africa*, Vol.I, Western Cape, Durban: Indicator Press.

McIntosh, A., Sibanda, S., Vaughan, A. and Th. Xaba, 1996, 'Traditional Authorities and Land

Reform in South Africa: Lessons from KwaZulu Natal', *Development Southern Africa*, Vol.13, No.3, June, pp.339–57.

Manona, Cecil, 1998, 'Rural Land Use and Tenure: A Case Study in the Eastern Cape', in *Proceedings of the International Conference on Land Tenure in the Developing World*, University of Cape Town, Cape Town, 25–27 Jan., pp.404–9.

Marcus, Tessa, Eales, Kath and Adele Wildschut, 1996, *Down to Earth: Land Demand in the New South Africa*, Durban: Indicator Press, University of Natal.

Masilela, C. and D. Weiner, 1996, 'Resettlement Planning in Zimbabwe and South Africa's Land Reform Discourse', *Third World Planning Review*, Vol.18, No.1, pp.23–43.

Mathye, Mihloti, 1997, 'Submission to the Land Reform Policy Committee', March, Pretoria.

Mbatha, Liphapha with Cathi Albertyn, 1997, 'Allocating Land to Women? A Study of the Practices in Taun and Braaklagte', Johannesburg, Report for the DLA, Feb., unpublished.

Meer, Shamin, 1997, 'Gender and Land Rights', *IDS Bulletin*, Vol.28, No.3, July, pp.133–44.

Meer, Shamin (ed.), 1997, *Women, Land and Authority: Perspectives from South Africa*, Oxford: Oxfam/David Phillips.

Middleton, Sue, 1997, 'Women's Land Rights and Needs: the Case of Thornhill and Merino Walk', in Meer (ed.) [*1997: 74–83*].

Mogale, Constance and Sophie Phohsoko, 1997, 'The Women's Rights in Land Workshop', *Agenda*, No.32, pp.66–8.

Murray, Colin, 1996, 'Land Reform in the Eastern Free State', in 'The Agrarian Question in South Africa', Special Issue of *The Journal of Peasant Studies*, Vol.23, Nos.2/3, pp.209–44.

Murray, Colin and Gavin Williams, 1994, 'Land and Freedom in South Africa', *Review of African Political Economy*, Vol.61, pp.316–24.

Palmer, Robin, 1996, 'The Threat to People's Land in Southern Africa: the Current Crisis', Briefing Paper, Oxford, Oxfam UK.

Pankhurst, Donna and Susie Jacobs, 1988, 'Land Tenure, Gender Relations and Agricultural Production: the Case of Zimbabwe's Peasantry', in J. Davison (ed.), *Women, Agriculture and Land*, Boulder, CO: Westview, pp.202–27.

Rai, Shirin, 1996, 'Women and Politics in the Third World: Some Issues for Debate', in S. Rai and G. Lievesley (eds.), *Women and the State: International Perspectives*, London: Taylor & Francis.

Seidman, G., 1993, 'No Freedom without the Women: Mobilisation and Gender in South Africa: 1970-92', *Signs*, Vol.18, No.2, pp.291–322.

Siqwana-Ndulo, Nombelelo, 1996, 'Can True Gender Equality be Realised in Land Redistribution in South Africa?', paper to the Committee for Family Research of the International Sociological Association, KwaZulu-Natal, July.

Small, Janet, 1997, 'Women's Land Rights: A Case Study from the Northern Transvaal', in Meer [*1997: 45–52*].

Sunde, Jackie and Johann Hamman, 1996, 'Entitled to What? Gender, Land Reform Policy and the Role of the Law in Mediating Access to Land', paper delivered to the Southern African Sociological Association Congress, Durban, July.

van Zyl, Johan and Hans Binswanger (eds.), 1996, *Agricultural Land Reform in South Africa*, Oxford/Cape Town: Oxford University Press.

van Zyl, Johan, 1996, 'A New Vision for Agriculture and Management of the Transition', in Johan van Zyl and Hans Binswanger (eds.), *Agricultural Land Reform in South Africa*, Oxford/Cape Town: Oxford University Press, pp.602–8.

Walker, Cherryl, 1994, 'Women, "Tradition" and Reconstruction', *Review of African Political Economy*, Vol.61, pp.347–58.

Walker, Cherryl, 1996, 'Reconstructing Tradition: Women and Land Reform', in P. Rich (ed.), *Reaction and Renewal in South Africa*, Basingstoke: Macmillan.

Walker, Cherryl, 1997, 'Cornfields, Gender and Land', in Meer (ed.) [*1997: 55–73*].

Williams, Gavin, 1996, 'Setting the Agenda: a Critique of the World Bank's Rural Restructuring Programme for South Africa', *Journal of Southern African Studies*, Vol.22, No.1.

Women's Human Rights and African Customary Laws: Between Universalism and Relativism – Individualism and Communitarianism

ANNE HELLUM

This contribution problematises the role of law in women's development in the light of universalist, culture relativist and pluralist perspectives on human rights. The management of procreative problems among different groups of women within the patrilineal Shona-speaking population in Zimbabwe demonstrates the dilemmas and conflicts that women's identities as individuals and as members of a family group are giving rise to in relation to law reform. A pluralist and processual position, which extends beyond the dichotomous perception of women as individuals versus women as members of a family group inherent in both the universalist and the relativist approach, is pointed out as the way forward. Rather than identifying the legal needs of women in general, the article demonstrates the importance of exploring both the general characteristics and unique features of social and legal relations.

INTRODUCTION

This contribution problematises the role of human rights in women's development in the African context, where membership in the new nation-state in terms of citizenship and membership of a family group are giving rise to different rights and obligations. My study of the management of procreative problems among the patrilineal Shona-speaking population in Zimbabwe, with particular reference to the use of polygynous procreative arrangements, serves as a departure point [*Hellum, 1998*]. Polygynous procreative arrangements are situated at the cutting-edge of the international obligation to eliminate discrimination against women in marriage on the one hand and the urge to respond to childless women's different, shifting and complex legal needs as individuals and as members of past, present and future generations on the other. In this article the dilemmas and conflicts that the rapid, complex and

---

Anne Hellum is Associate Professor, Institute of Women's Law, University of Oslo.

uneven socio-legal development is giving rise to in relation to law reform affecting different groups of childless women in Zimbabwe are discussed in the light of universalist, culture relativist and pluralist perspectives on human rights. A pluralist and processual position, which extends beyond the dichotomous perception of women as individuals versus women as members of a family group inherent in both the universalist and the relativist approach, is pointed out as the way forward.

COEXISTING PROCREATIVE NORMS AT THE LOCAL, NATIONAL AND INTERNATIONAL LEVEL

The UN Convention on the Elimination of All Forms of Discrimination against Women (the Women's Convention), which is ratified by more than 150 states, has laid the foundation for an international women's law of human rights that transcends the borders of national, religious and customary laws. It sets out to ensure the right of every woman to health (Article 12), education (Article 10), work (Article 11), political participation (Articles 7–8), credit facilities (Article 13) and to marry, to found a family and to divorce (Article 16) on an equal basis with men. The social, cultural, economic and legal differences between the countries that have ratified the Women's Convention have given rise to a series of problems as regards its implementation [*Armstrong et al., 1993; Oloka-Onyango and Tamale, 1995; Nhlapo, 1989; Stewart and Ncube et al., 1997*]. This article addresses some of the inconsistencies and contradictions which the implementation of the non-discrimination principle is giving rise to in relation to people's management of procreative problems in different localities in Zimbabwe.

Among the Shona-speaking population in Zimbabwe family-based customs, aimed at ensuring generational continuity through the patrilineage, co-exist with an increasingly individualistic, gender- and fertility-neutral family law. In their management of procreative problems people resort to remedies ranging from family-based arrangements like polygynous procreative unions and fluctuating custody arrangements to modern solutions like anonymous adoption and artificial fertilisation. Remedies like modern adoption and artificial insemination by donor is met with resistance because the blood-ties between the child and its biological father are disrupted. In a situation where the well-being of the child is seen as linked to protection by the spirits of the forefathers, people prefer measures like fluctuating custody arrangements and polygynous marriage arrangements.

To measure the progress made as regards implementing the Women's Convention within this area of life and law, I have explored decision-making in the family, in spiritual mediation by traditional healers and in mediation by the community court. To come to grips with the factors and forces which affect the way in which the new family and marriage laws interact with local procreative norms and values, such as the patrilineal bloodline principle, in different contexts and settings I have carried out fieldwork among 1) Christian elite women in Harare 2) lower class women from Chitungwiza urban area and 3) peasant women from Seke rural area. The way in which people choose between these different options has provided insight into the ongoing process of interplay between coexisting procreative norms, values and perceptions.

My study shows that Christian elite women from the urban upper classes are in a better position than poor rural women with regards to making use of the increasingly individualistic, fertility-neutral and egalitarian marriage laws. It also shows how the plurality of identities and affiliations inherent in each and every woman and man 'force' each one to compromise constantly between individualistic and communalistic norms and values in pursuit of solutions to their procreative problems. Most women who face procreative problems turn both to traditional healers and to modern doctors. Their commitment as members of a church community is usually combined with active participation in a patrilineal extended family who on occasions like marriage, birth and death establish contact with their ancestral spirits.

In its response to international human rights and people's procreative coping strategies, Zimbabwe – like other countries in the process of modernisation – is trapped between individualistic and communitarian family forms, norms and values. The Zimbabwean marriage regime represents a compromise between the recognition of cultural multiplicity and legal pluralism on the one hand, and the aim of gender equality and legal unification on the other. The recognition of a polygamous procreative union depends on what kind of marriage the parties have contracted. A civil marriage under the Marriage Act is a monogamous union regardless of whether the husband has paid *lobolo* to his wife's family or not. A woman or man who is validly married under a monogamous system under general law cannot contract a second marriage [*Ncube, 1989: 139; Feltoe, 1989: 62–4*]. A registered customary marriage under the Customary Marriages Act is potentially polygamous. A man who is married under this act may contract one or more further marriages under the same Act. A woman does not have a similar right to contract a second marriage.

Whether and to what extent Zimbabwe's plural marriage and family law regime should be replaced by a uniform system is today a contested issue. On the one hand, legal unification and abolition of polygamy by law, may imply that procreative entitlements and obligations guaranteed by membership of the family group are being fragmented or undermined. On the other hand, the recognition of family based procreative customs and practices may have the effect of violating women's right to equality and self-determination. As pointed out in this article the universalist, the relativist and the pluralist positions offer different solutions to these dilemmas and conflicts.

THE UNIVERSALIST AND CENTRALIST POSITION

Universalism is a position that is interested in the similarities between human beings, groups and situations regardless of their different social and cultural contexts. The proponents of universality claim that international human rights like gender equality, self-determination and freedom are and must be the same everywhere. The universalist human rights position assumes that inalienable rights exist above those in power and regardless of time and space. According to Cranston:

> A human right by definition is a universal moral right, something which all men, everywhere, at all times ought to have, something of which no one may be deprived without a grave affront to justice, something which is owing to every human being simply because he is human [*Cranston, 1973: 36*].

The universalist position is closely related to centralist legal theory which is the dominant doctrinal position in Western legal science. Within this tradition different norms and values are seen as incommensurable. The problem of difference is resolved on the basis of the idea of the existence of overriding norms and values. In line with a monist perception of law, coherence and harmony between different norms and values is ensured through the establishment of an hierarchy of values and sources.

A major issue in the liberal political and philosophical discussion about women's rights and human rights in Africa is the apparent incommensurability of individual and collective rights [*Howard, 1990: 159–84; 1992: 97–9*]. From such a perspective women's identities as members of an extended family network are often regarded as a major obstacle to the implementation of women's human rights.

> Considering the strong identification that women have with kinship structures and the family, they may not want to struggle for the essential rights that they should have as a citizen in society, as a person in themselves, particularly in modern states where everybody's human rights are being trampled upon'[*Center for Women's Global Leadership, 1994: 11*].

My study of the use of polygynous procreative unions in Zimbabwe shows the different needs and interests of childless women and men and from different groups of the Shona population. While polygynous procreative marriage unions are still common among large segments of the rural population, they are losing their significance in urban areas. While an urban childless first wife often prefers a monogamous union, the woman who gets involved in an informal procreative union wants to secure her position through marital status.

It is a problematic relationship between the uneven and complex development taking place on the ground and the universalist position which assumes that individualistic values and principles always take precedence over communitarian values.

The plurality of norms and values that exist in different cultures and societies are also reflected within the human rights system itself. The human rights system embodies both individual and communal rights. There is, for example, a tense relationship between the principle of a group's self determination and cultural identity as embodied in the African Charter on Human and People's Rights (the Charter) and Article 16.1 of the Women's Convention, which puts an obligation on states to eliminate discrimination against women in all matters relating to marriage and family relations. Of particular interest in the African context is whether the protection of group rights, such as the cultural and religious identity of an ethnic group, constitutes a justifiable reason for differential treatment of women and men.

Regardless of the existing cultural and legal diversity, human rights theory holds that the consideration of violations of the non-discrimination principle must, like other human rights principles and in line with practice of international human rights bodies, be determined in the light of uniformly held international standards [*Cook, 1994: 234–5*]. The general view of the Human Rights Committee has a bearing on the interpretation of the non-discrimination standard in the Women's Convention.

> Its interpretation and application of the International Covenant on Civil and Political Rights has to be based on the principle that the terms and concepts of the Covenant are independent of any particular national system of law and of all dictionary definitions. Although the terms of the Covenant are derived from long traditions within many nations, the Committee must now regard them as having an autonomous meaning [*UN Document CCPR/C/DR, 1982: para.10.2*].

In its interpretation of Article 16.1 (c) of the Women's Convention which lays down that women and men shall have 'the same rights and responsibilities during marriage and at its dissolution', the Committee on the Elimination of All Forms of Discrimination against Women (CEDAW) has seen polygynous procreative arrangements which allow men to take a second wife while women are allowed to take only one husband as a contravention. In questions and comments on country reports, the CEDAW Committee has on a number of occasions commented on the discriminatory nature of polygyny. In its review of Senegal's report, the CEDAW Committee paid particular attention to the relationship between legislation, customary law and Islamic law.[1] It asked what steps were being taken to intensify and modify discriminatory customs and practices in connection with polygamy [*CEDAW, 1988, A/43/38, para.567*]. In connection with the Fourth World Conference on Women which was held in Beijing in 1995, CEDAW prepared a report called the Report of the Committee on Progress Achieved in the Implementation of the Convention. The Draft Report, which was prepared by the Secretariat on the basis of the country reports, addresses polygamous marriage in connection with Article 16. According to the Draft Report,

> State Parties' reports also disclose that polygamy is practised in a number of countries. Polygamous marriage contravenes a woman's right to equality with men, and can have such serious emotional and financial consequences for her and her dependants that such marriages ought to be discouraged and prohibited. The Committee notes with concern that some States Parties, whose constitutions guarantee equal rights, permit polygamous marriage in accordance with personal or customary law. This violates the constitutional rights of women, and breaches the provisions of article 5 (a) of the Convention [*CEDAW/C/1995/7: 109*].

My study questions the adequacy of the abolition of polygyny by law for different women who live under different socio-legal circumstances. Joseph's case is illustrative of the consequences that the simplistic abolitionist approach may have for different groups of women in a situation where individual and communal procreative forms, norms and values coexist.

> Joseph married his first wife in 1942. His first wife was barren. In 1949 Joseph married another wife whom he had two children with. This marriage was dissolved in 1956. Joseph told Chavunduka that he found it difficult as a Christian to continue with his second marriage. The children were adopted by his first wife. Joseph rejoined the church in order to become an active member of the Moral Rearmament Association [*Chavunduka, 1979: 46*].

Like Joseph many Christian men's identity is still linked to their procreative capacity. As a response to new knowledge and changing living conditions they try to reconcile the new with the old. According to Chavunduka's observations in St. Mary's township in Chitungwiza, many Christian men who have an urge to have children on the one hand and fear of the church's condemnation of polygyny on the other, try to find ways of producing children without abandoning their Christian faith and breaking the law [*Chavunduka, 1979: 44–6*]. Some men, he observed, took leave of absence from the church to devote some years of their life to producing children. Temporary marriage arrangements were made towards this end. These marriages were sometimes dissolved when the man had achieved his objective of producing a reasonable number of children.

The shift from the use of formal to informal polygynous procreative unions have important implications for both the first wife, the childbearing woman and the child. Women who have entered into informal procreative unions are in a particularly vulnerable position when the man wants to pull out of the relationship and take custody of the child. In the course of my fieldwork I came across several incidents where the mother had consented to such arrangements because she could not afford to maintain her child. As she had neither entered a modern civil nor a recognised customary marriage she was without legal protection when the union was dissolved. The interests of the first wife were also overlooked. In Chitungwiza high density area I came across a number of incidents where the man had entered into an informal union without consulting his childless first wife.

The informal procreative arrangements that are mushrooming in the gap between a uniform marriage law assuming free and equal individuals and the customary law regarding a marriage as a contract between two families constitute a new form of female exploitation that did not exist customarily. On the basis of this background, the conclusion reached by this study is that modernisation has not changed the status of women in Zimbabwe to the extent that only 'modern' legal strategies can solve the problems confronted by childless women in the process of marriage and divorce.

THE RELATIVIST POSITION

Unlike the universalist position, the culture-relativist approach regards different value systems as unique and incomparable units. Unlike universalists, culture relativists deny that conflicts between values from different traditions can be settled in any reasonable way. What is reasonable is itself a product of particular cultures and societies. Overriding standards for the resolution of value conflicts do not exist. It is a position which emphasises the uniqueness of all human beings, groups and social situations. It assumes that every society, law and culture is a unique and incomparable unit which should be understood in its own right.

Cultural relativism was initially a theory that questioned the eurocentric notions of civilisation and progress which placed the Western world with its economic and legal systems at the top of the evolutionary ladder [Renteln, 1990: 61–87]. Cultural relativism was cast as a value theory which aimed to achieve greater equality and greater understanding of the different cultures and societies of the world.

> We shall arrive at a more realistic social faith, accepting as grounds for hope and as new bases for tolerance the coexisting and equally valid patterns of life which mankind has created for itself from the raw material of existence [Benedict, 1934: 278].

An important aspect of cultural relativism today is that it challenges the universality of standards which actually belong to one culture. Proponents of the communalist argument have contended that human rights presuppose a society which is atomised and individualistic. Extreme proponents of this viewpoint have even claimed that individual human rights are irrelevant in Africa, since neither men nor women normally view themselves as individuals but as members of various social groups, such as the family, the clan or the tribe. For this reason much scholarly and legal attention has been paid to the human rights instruments that protect the rights of groups, with particular emphasis on the groups' right to self-determination and cultural integrity.[2] Underlying this approach emphasising the uniqueness of different societies and cultures is the assumption that African norms and values are incompatible with the norms and values applied in the West.

The conception of the ethnic or social group as a unique and incomparable unit has often implied that women's quest for equality and self-determination has been overlooked or occupied a marginal and inferior position. The reason is that the family or the ethnic group has been seen as an entity made up of members who are assumed to have common goals.[3] Recent studies of gender and legal pluralism in former British colonies in Africa have rectified this ideal picture of the ethnic or social group as a closed entity with a consistent and coherent system of norms, values and interests. A number of historical studies on gender and legal change show how African women, through their quest for better living conditions, have sought alliances that cut across membership of family, ethnicity and class [Rwezaura, 1990: 17; Parpart, 1988: 134; Schmidt, 1992]. Although women have often joined forces with men over issues such as strikes and guerrilla warfare, it has been conflicts concerning marital behaviour that have dominated their daily lives.

By applying a gender perspective we clearly see that custom and culture does not constitute a unified corpus of symbols and meanings which can be definitely interpreted but is contested, temporal and emergent [Clifford, 1986: 19; Moore, 1994: 364]. The confused situation as regards the customary procedures surrounding a polygynous procreative union is illustrative. According to written sources of customary law a man is supposed to consult his first wife and his family if he wants to take a second wife for procreative purposes. In the urban areas many men enter into informal procreative unions without consulting their wives. They assert that it is their right to have a girlfriend or a second wife for procreative purposes. Many women feel that the men's way of addressing the problem is an abuse of power and not a matter of custom. Whether the customary obligation to consult has broken down and is being replaced by a new norm is a question depending on a number of factors. It is necessary to consider just how widespread the new norm is in social, institutional and gendered space. The fact that women disagree with the men's

version throws doubt on the normative legitimacy of the new practice, as does
the fact that childless women who want to maintain their marriage often feel
obliged to accept such solutions because they are in a weak bargaining
position.

This example illustrates the shortcomings of the culture relativist position
in women's law studies in contemporary African society. The uncontaminated
and harmonious small scale societies whose members possess a coherent
identity no longer exist. In a situation where a wide range of international,
legislated and customary norms and values together with practical
considerations fit strategic individuals with conflicting interests, the culture
relativist paradigm for the resolution of value conflicts, namely that what is
reasonable is itself a product of particular cultures and societies, seems an
impossible path to pursue. I thus agree with the human rights researcher Jack
Donnelly who has emphasised the need to consider the socio-cultural basis for
cultural relativism in a changing world. In his view, what we see in the Third
World today is often not:

> the persistence of traditional culture in the face of modern intrusions, or
> even the development of syncretic cultures and values, but rather a
> disruptive 'Westernization', cultural confusion, or the enthusiastic
> embrace of 'modern' practices and values. In other words, the traditional
> culture advanced to justify cultural relativism far too often no longer
> exists [*Donnelly, 1989: 118*].

In a situation where a wide range of international and legislated norms are
merged with local norms, perceptions and values in complex chains of human
relationships there is, as demonstrated by my study, a basis for dialogue and
change.

PLURALIST, PROCESSUAL AND CONTEXTUAL ALTERNATIVES

In an attempt to reconcile conflicting human rights values like gender equality
and cultural diversity in a dynamic, flexible and situation-sensitive manner, the
emerging pluralist alternative seeks to define a space between universalism
and relativism as well as individualism and communalism. Proponents of
cultural pluralism argue that it offers a via media – a space between
universalism and cultural relativism – and places conflicting values within a
cultural context while simultaneously giving room for dialogue and change
[*Freeman, 1997*].[4] Pluralists recognise the existence of primary values.
Pluralists accept that conflicts among primary values can be resolved by
appealing to some reasonable ranking of the values in question. As regards
conflicts between human rights values like gender equality and the protection
of culture and custom the answer lies in analysing the conflicting values in the

social and cultural context in which the individuals concerned live and act.

The Space for Pluralism in Human Rights Doctrine

Human rights doctrine offers a space for pluralism. The way in which the balance between university and diversity is drawn in terms of a combination of autonomous and contextual interpretation and implementation of human rights instruments illustrates this point. As far as the formulation of the obligation of the States Parties to implement the Women's Convention is concerned, the concept 'appropriate measures' in Article 2 provides leeway to take social, cultural and economic differences into consideration. In its analysis of Article 2 of the Convention the Secretariat[5] to the CEDAW Committee concluded that:

> The Convention allows for the interpretation and application in the most appropriate ways to the social and cultural structure of each state but with the premise that the States Parties will follow the principle of non-discrimination on the basis of sex [*CEDAW C/1995/4: para.105*].

Similar viewpoints are held by the Committee on Economic, Social and Cultural Rights:

> the phrase 'by all appropriate means' must be given its full and natural meaning. While each state party must decide for itself which means are the most appropriate under the circumstances with respect to each of the rights, the 'appropriateness' of the means chosen will not always be self-evident. It is therefore desirable that States Parties' reports should indicate not only the measures that have been taken but also the basis on which they are considered to be the most 'appropriate' under the circumstances [*UN Doc.E/1991/23, para.4*].

To structure customary laws by legislative and judicial intervention, or to create a procedural framework that allows customary law to evolve in response to the ongoing process of legal, social, economic and cultural change, are two different, yet often interrelated legal strategies, both of which have been pursued by the African States Parties to the Women's Convention. The pluralist position, which allows customary law to evolve in a situation-sensitive manner, has been coined by both African and Western legal scholars. Professor Albie Sachs, Judge of the Constitutional Court in South Africa, has drawn attention to the conflicts and dilemmas faced by lawmakers and judges regarding the resolution of the conflict between women's right to equality and the protection of family and culture embodied in the new South African Constitution.[6] As an alternative to the establishment of a value hierarchy Sachs envisages a community and rights-based law which in a situation-sensitive manner may combine the justice of the individual case with the human dignity of the parties.

In my view, there is a need for empirical insight into the efficacy of these strategies for improving the position of different groups of women in different contexts and settings. My study of the management of procreative problems in marriage and divorce in Zimbabwe has enabled me to make some empirically grounded suggestions as to how adequately measures, such as the abolition of discriminatory procreative practices and the harmonisation of different norms and values, undertaken by the local courts represent the socio-legal reality of women from different groups.

Contextualising Value Conflicts: Some Case Studies

My study of the management of procreative problems in the process of marriage illustrates the dilemmas and contradictions besetting the process of law reform in relation to the abolition of discriminatory customary laws and practices in a situation where the interests, needs and values of women who are situated differently in terms of age, class and marital status come into conflict. Regardless of their right to equality, large groups of childless women resort to polygynous procreative arrangements. In the rural areas of Zimbabwe it is not uncommon for a childless wife to ask the husband to take a younger sister as a second wife for procreative purposes. In the urban centres polygamous marriage arrangements are, however, being replaced by informal procreative unions. Middle and upper class women often resist such arrangements whilst childbearing women want to enhance the status of the unions they have entered into.

How relevant the abolition of polygyny by law is for the socio-legal reality of different women who are involved in polygynous procreative arrangements is an important issue for international human rights bodies, states parties and NGOs aiming to improve the position of women. In the context of Zimbabwe's complex, uneven and multi-level legal landscape we need to analyse the differential impact of such a reform on men and women and on women from different age groups and different social groupings. In Zimbabwe the existing prohibition against polygyny in civil marriages constitutes a resource in the hands of women who want to secure their position as the sole wife. It responds to the values and lifestyle of women from the Christian middle and upper class [*Weinrich, 1982: 72*]. It is the shortest path from an uncertain and negotiable position to a secure and predictable situation. The following Supreme Court case illustrates the efficacy of this type of regulation for protecting the interests of the childless first wife.

> In his appeal from the maintenance court at Murewa the husband, who was ordered to pay $60 per month as maintenance for his childless wife, contended that he was not liable to pay maintenance because his wife wrongfully and unlawfully had deserted him. The husband argued that

his wife by accepting the second 'wife' had abandoned her divorce rights. He had wanted to ask one of her nieces to come as his second wife but that had failed: I then told her I was going to get another wife and we agreed. I found one, consulted her and she told me she was not happy about her and I abandoned her. I then looked for a girl and had a child. After we had stayed for some time, she said love cannot be shared and said [she] was going back to her home. The husband's attempt of playing off the negotiative rationality that dominates the family setting on the court arena was not successful. The Supreme Court found evidence that the wife had left her husband for a combination of two reasons; that her husband took a second 'wife', maltreated her and ordered her to leave. The husband's attitude was seen as clearly contrary to public policy and destructive of the basis of Christian marriage [*Supreme Court of Zimbabwe, case no.54/87*].

It is important, however, to keep in mind that the Marriage Act, with its one-dimensional construction of relationships, silences the voice of the childbearing woman. In order to provide a full picture we must also pay attention to the fora that deal with the situation of the childbearing woman who as a result of the prohibition against polygyny has entered into an informal procreative union. Chavunduka's study of the Makoni Tribal Court in St. Mary's Township offers insight into a number of cases where parties to informal unions sought divorce. The Makoni Tribal Court, which met every Sunday, was headed by headman Makoni. Its proceedings were informal. In some instances a union was seen as binding, regardless of whether a bride-price had been paid. In other cases the parties were reconciled and the man was ordered to pay bride wealth [*Chavunduka, 1979: Case No.2, 25.9.77*]. At the Makoni Court a mother had a right of action against a man who was unwilling to let his children take his surname by a 'mapoto marriage' [*Chavunduka, 1979: Case No.3, 16.10.77*]. Through a flexible and situational conception of marriage, women who have entered into informal procreative unions were rendered some protection. A major consideration cutting across these cases was to protect women and children from men's strategic manipulations which constructed relationships in such a manner that they did not give rise to responsibilities under customary law. In this situation the need to protect women and to ensure that men accepted their responsibilities was seen as more important than equality between autonomous individuals.

Insight into the reconciliatory practice of urban and rural community courts shows how presiding officers of the semi-professional community courts try to combine customary values, such as marital stability and the protection of women, with the new gender values emphasising gender equality and individual autonomy [*Cutshall, 1991*]. The community court, which constitutes the lowest level of the formal court hierarchy, has the power to reconcile matrimonial disputes in registered customary marriages. Judicial proceedings aim to produce amicable settlements which restore social harmony within the community. Some community court presiding officers reject divorce complaints from the husband which are based on the barrenness of the wife. They are of the view that such claims have no basis in customary law, since the husband has the right to marry another wife, either from the wife's family or elsewhere. Most of the community court presiding officers, however, direct the parties to a family remedy agent or a medical practitioner. According to an urban community court presiding officer:

> We usually try to persuade them to live together, develop other interests, or adopt a child from the Social Welfare Department. And some couples do go on to live happily without children. But this requires a very understanding and enlightened man [*Cutshall, 1991: 204*].

Some community-court presiding officers feel that a woman's childbearing capacity is becoming less important in modern society, particularly in view of the growing concern about a 'population boom' and its impact upon national economic growth and the general standard of living [*Cutshall, 1991: 204*]. In the following case from Seke Community Court, the presiding officer explicitly states that childlessness is no barrier to reconciliation.

> Since the parties have agreed to resolve their differences and agreed to reconciliation the court encourage them for tolerance towards each other. What might be straining their love and happiness is the reason that since Nicholas was borne 15 years ago, she has not given birth. But both parties did not accept it was the major cause of their misunderstanding. I see no reason why they should not reconcile as they still love each other (Seke Community Court).

These different levels of dispute resolution have much in common with what de Sousa Santos [*1987: 287–91*] has termed different scales of legality. While they regulate the same kind of social activity (in our case the use of polygynous procreative arrangements) they use different criteria to determine the relevant features of the activity to be regulated. The Supreme Court is guided by a rule-oriented approach characterised by its narrow relevance criteria. Unlike the Supreme Court, the urban headman's court contextualises behaviour in its immediate surroundings and is sensitive to complex relations. From a situational women's perspective the different levels of legality do not necessarily constitute separate and conflicting normative systems. They may, under the circumstances, supplement each other in a way that caters for the needs and interests of differently situated women within complex procreative relationships. Therefore, a general prohibition against sex-discrimination combined with a pluralistic marriage regime may, under the circumstances, be preferable to wholesale solutions such as abolition of polygyny by law.

FUTURE OF WOMEN'S HUMAN RIGHTS RESEARCH: BOTH SAMENESS AND DIFFERENCE

In my study of the management of procreative problems in marriage and divorce a major concern has been how to conceptualise and interpret women's use of individual rights and reciprocal family relationships. The conflicts and dilemmas which the application of the Women's Convention is generating in a socially, culturally and legally diverse world has demonstrated the need for a theory of interpretation 'which extends its aim beyond the legal text and towards the various contexts of the text' [*Dahl, 1988: 2*]. While the dogmatic doctrine of interpretation of human rights law is necessary for its purpose (i.e. to safeguard the interests of women who are in a social and economic position to make use of their equal rights), a wider approach enhances the understanding of how women's human rights function in relation to different groups of women in various contemporary contexts.[7] Rather than being mutually exclusive the two sets of interpretative theories may deepen our understanding of complex socio-legal phenomena.

My study demonstrates that simplistic and one-dimensional dichotomies, such as communal versus individualistic, male versus female, Western versus African, traditional versus modern and folk law versus state-law, do not help in understanding how procreative gender relationships are constituted in the process of complex and uneven social and legal change. This implies rejecting both universalist theories, based on abstract notions of gender equality, and relativist theories, which assume harmonious and balanced societies based on complementary gender roles, in favour of 'grounded theories' based on empirical studies of how gender relations are constituted in specific situations and processes.[8]

By adopting an empirical and experiential starting point in a social, legal and cultural context which differed from my own, the need to extend the aim of interpretation beyond generalised assumptions about women's common needs and values became evident. This was the dominant perspective in Norwegian women's law in the 1980s, represented by Dahl:

> Considerations of justice in women's law start by identifying the needs and wants of women *in general*, and particularly opinions about what is just. Out of this matrix of needs and opinions we may develop a series of hypotheses about values on the basis of which we wish to study and examine the law. We then allow the individual legal rules and sets of rules to confront these values and the principles derived from these

values. This provides a foundation for new hypotheses about the compatibility or incompatibility of the legal rules and the derived principles, which are then tested, on the basis of our own experiences and women's presumed needs, wants and notions of justice [*Dahl, 1987: 90*].

Rather than identifying the legal needs of women in general my study demonstrates the importance of exploring both the general characteristics and unique features of social and legal relations. The identification of similarities makes it possible to make generalisations concerning women's common values and interests within a limited span of time and place. Unique cases are important because they point to variations and question the validity of our tentative generalisations concerning women's common needs and interests.

NOTES

1. Senegal's initial report CEDAW/C/5/Add.42 and the additional report CEDAW/C/5/Add.42/Amend. 1 were considered at CEDAW's seventh session in 1988, A/43/38.
2. *The Rights of Peoples* edited by James Crawford [*1988*] is conspicuous for its silence on gender relations. In the collection of articles edited by Morse and Woodman [1988] and Allott and Woodman [1985] women, where mentioned at all, are seen as part of the indigenous group. One such example is Bell [*1988: 297–313*].
3. The Norwegian anthropologists Howell and Melhuus [*1993*] make the point that anthropological studies of kinship have failed to come to grips with the gender dimension.
4. A number of authors are currently striving to create an intermediate space for the mutual criticism and enrichment of Western and non-Western legal cultures. In his article 'Problems of Universal Legitimacy for Human Rights' the legal scholar Abdullahi Ahmed An-Na'im [*An-Na'im and Deng, 1990: 331–68*] emphasises the role of cross-cultural human rights dialogue with regard to creating, interpreting and implementing human rights. In *The Best Interest of the Child, Reconciling Culture and Human Rights* Philip Alston [*1994: 2*] maintains that there is a need to 'inject an element of specificity which will facilitate a much deeper appreciation of the complexity of the issues, at the same time as pointing the way towards approaches which involve neither the embrace of an artificial and sterile universalism nor the acceptance of an ultimately self-defeating cultural relativism'. In 'Anti-Essentialism, Relativism, and Human Rights', Tracy Higgins [*1996: 125–7*] concludes that forging a combined strategy which respects both commonality and difference requires feminists to acknowledge that they cannot eliminate the risk of coercion altogether, but the risk of inaction is also present.
5. At its twelfth session, the CEDAW Committee requested the Secretariat to prepare, as a pre-session document, an analysis of Article 2 of the Convention, in the light of reports of States Parties and other sources [*CEDAW/C/1995/4*]. As of February 1997, the CEDAW Committee hoped to place an analysis of Article 2 on the agenda of a future session.
6. Albie Sach's keynote speech was given to the 9th World Conference of the International Society of Family Law on 'Changing Family Forms: World Themes and African Issues' held in Durban in 1997.
7. In international feminist jurisprudence Hilary Charlesworth [*1994: 61*] emphasises that, although acquisition of rights is by no means the only solution to the world-wide domination of women by men, it is an important tactic in the international arena. As women in most societies operate from a disadvantaged position, rights discourse offers a recognised vocabulary for framing political and social wrongs. Martha Minow [*1987: 1860–919*] addresses the problems caused by the denial by feminist jurisprudence of rights discourse to traditionally dominated groups: 'I worry about criticising rights and legal language just when they have become available to people who have previously lacked access to them. I worry about those who have,

telling those who do not, "you do not need it, you do not want it".'
8. On 'grounded theory' in legal research see Bentzon, Hellum, Stewart, Ncube and Agersnap
[*1998*].

REFERENCES

Allott, A. and G.R. Woodman (eds.), 1985, *People's Law and State Law: The Bellagio Papers*, Dordrecht: Foris Publications.

Alston, P. (ed.), 1994, *The Best Interest of the Child, Reconciling Culture and Human Rights*, Oxford: Oxford University Press.

An-Na'im, A. A. and F. M. Deng (eds.), 1990, *Human Rights in Africa, Cross-Cultural Perspectives*, Washington, DC: The Brookings Institution.

Armstrong, A. *et al.*, 1993, 'Excavating Women's Rights in African Family Law', *International Journal of Law and Family*, Vol.7, pp.314-69.

Bell, D., 1988, 'Aboriginal Women and the Recognition of Customary Law in Australia', in Morse and Woodman (eds.) [*1988*].

Benedict, R., 1934, *Patterns of Culture*, Boston, MA: Houghton Mifflin.

Bentzon, A. W., Hellum, A., J. Stewart, J., Ncube, W. and T. Agersnap, 1998, *Pursuing Grounded Theory in Law: South-North Experiences in Building Women's Law*, Oslo: TANO.

CEDAW, 1988, A/43/38, 'Report of the Committee on the Elimination of Discrimination against Women', Seventh Session.

CEDAW/C/1995/4, 'Implementation of Article 21 of the Convention on the Elimination of All Forms of Discrimination Against Women', Report of the Secretariat.

CEDAW/C/1995/7, 'Contributions of the Committee to International Conferences', Report of the Committee on progress achieved in the implementation of the Convention, Note by the Secretariat.

CEDAW, A/CONF. 177/7, 'Progress Achieved in the Implementation of the Convention on the Elimination of All Forms of Discrimination against Women, report by the Committee on the Elimination of Discrimination against Women.

Center for Women's Global Leadership, 1994, 'Gender Violence and Women's Human Rights in Africa', mimeo.

Charlesworth, H., 1994, 'What are Women's International Human Rights?', in R. Cook (ed.) [*1994*].

Chavunduka, G.L., 1979, 'A Shona Urban Court', *Mambo Occasional Papers Socio-Economic Series*, No.14. Gweru: Mambo Press.

Clifford, J., 1986, *The Predicament of Culture: Twentieth-century Ethnography, Literature and Art*, Cambridge, MA: Harvard University Press.

Cook, J., 1994, 'State Accountability Under the Convention on the Elimination of All Forms of Discrimination Against Women', in R. Cook (ed.) [*1994*].

Cook, R. (ed.), 1994, *Human Rights of Women, National and International Perspectives*, Philadelphia, PA: University of Pennsylvania Press.

Cranston, M., 1973, *What are Human Rights?* (2nd Edition), London: Bodley Head.

Crawford, J. (ed.), 1988, *The Rights of Peoples*, Oxford: Clarendon Press.

Cutshall, R.C. (1991), *Justice for the People, Community Courts and Legal Transformation in Zimbabwe*, Harare: University of Zimbabwe Publications.

Dahl, T.S., 1987, *Women's Law, An Introduction to Feminist Jurisprudence*, Oslo: Norwegian University Press.

Dahl, T.S., 1988, 'Towards an Interpretative Theory of Law – The Argument of Women's Law', in 'Methodology of Women's Law', *Studies in Women's Law*, No.7, University of Oslo.

Donnelly, J., 1989, *Universal Human Rights in Theory and Practice*, Ithaca, NY: Cornell University Press.

Feltoe, G., 1989, *A Guide to Zimbabwean Criminal Law*, Harare: Legal Resources Foundation.

Freeman, M., 1997, 'Cultural Pluralism and the Rights of the Child', in M. Freeman, *The Moral Status of Children*, Leiden: Martinus Nijhoff Publishers.

Hellum, A., 1998, 'Women's Human Rights and the Dynamics of African Customary Laws in a Changing World: Three Studies of Procreative Problems, Generational Continuity and Gender

Equality in Zimbabwean Family Law and Practice', (Doctoral thesis, Faculty of Law, University of Oslo in October 1997), Oslo: TANO.

Higgins, T.E., 1996, 'Anti Essentialism, Relativism and Human Rights', *Harvard Women's Law Journal*, Vol.19, pp.89–127.

Howard, R.E., 1990, 'Group versus Individual Identity in the African Debate on Human Rights', in An-Na'im and Deng (eds.) [*1990*].

Howard, R.E., 1992, 'Dignity, Community and Human Rights', in A.A. An-Na'im (ed.), *Human Rights in Cross-Cultural Perspective, A Quest for Consensus*, Philadelphia, PA: University of Pennsylvania Press.

Howell, S. and M. Melhuus, 1993, 'The Study of Kinship, the Study of Person; a Study of Gender?', in T. del Valle (ed.), *Gendered Anthropology*, London: Routledge.

Minow, M., 1987, 'Interpreting Rights: An Essay for Robert Cover', *Yale Law Journal*, Vol.96, pp.1860–910.

Moore, S.F., 1994, 'The Ethnography of the Present and the Analysis of Process', in R. Borofsky (ed.), *Assessing Cultural Anthropology*, New York: McGraw Hill.

Morse, B.W. and G.R. Woodman (eds.), 1988, *Indigenous Law and the State*, Dordrecht, Foris Publications.

Ncube, W., 1989, *Family Law in Zimbabwe*, Harare: Legal Resources Foundation.

Nhlapo, T.R., 1989, 'International Protection of Human Rights and the Family: African Variations on a Common Theme', *International Journal of Law and the Family*, Vol.3, pp.1–20.

Oloka-Onyango, J. and S. Tamale, 1995, 'The Personal is Political, or Why Women's Rights are Indeed Human Rights: An African Perspective on International Feminism', *Human Rights Quarterly*, Vol.17, pp.691–731.

Parpart, J., 1988, 'Sexuality and Power on the Zambian Copperbelt: 1926–1964', in S.B. Sticher and J.L. Parpart (eds.), *Patriarchy and Class in Africa*, Boulder, CO and London: Westview Press.

Renteln, A.D., 1990, *International Human Rights, Universalism Versus Relativism*, London: Sage Publication.

Rezaura, B., 1990, 'Researching on the Law of the Family in Tanzania: Some Reflections on Method, Theory and Limits of Law as a Tool for Social Change', in A. Armstrong (ed.), *Perspectives in Research Methodology*, Harare: Women and Law in Southern Africa, Research Project Working Paper No.2.

Santos, Boaventura de Sousa, 1987, 'Law: A Map of Misreading, Toward a Postmodern Conception of Law', *Journal of Law and Society*, Vol.14, No.3, pp.279–99.

Schmidt, E., 1992, *Peasants Traders and Wives, Shona Women in the History of Zimbabwe, 1870–1939*, Harare: Baobab Books.

Stewart, J. and W. Ncube et al., 1997, *Standing at the Cross Roads, WLSA and the Rights Dilemma Which Way Do We Go?*, Harare: Women and Law in Southern Africa Research Trust.

Weinrich, A.K.H., 1982, *African Marriage in Zimbabwe*, Gweru: Mambo Press.

UN Doc. CCPR/C/DR, 1982, Views of the Human Rights Committee, 7 April, in the Matter of Van Duzen v Canada, Communication No.R. 12/50.

UN Doc. E/1991/23, The Committee on Economic, Social and Cultural Rights, UN, GAOR, 5th session.

The Interplay between Collective Rights and Obligations and Individual Rights

RIE ODGAARD and AGNETE WEIS BENTZON

This essay argues that law should not be seen as a set of norms and principles which is independent from the social context. Its focus is on the different relationship, between rights and obligations in formal law and in living law. This is illustrated by examples from Tanzania and Greenland which show that imposed Western legal ideas have contributed to the disintegration of the most fundamental values by pursuing individual interests at the expense of consideration of the collective. The essay also examines how the relationship between individual and collective rights and obligations is defined by the interplay of formal law and living law in specific socio-cultural settings.

INTRODUCTION

The idea of individual human rights emerged in the Western World with the development of the democratic nation state and its transformation from a liberal state to the welfare or interventionist state [*Bottomley et al., 1994*]. The growth in the Western world of the idea of individual liberty rights must be seen against the background of earlier absolutism. It is at first a restriction on governmental power. Individual liberty rights and political rights attend and support the development of capitalism and representative democracy. Such rights can be claimed by every citizen *vis-à-vis* the state. Social and economic human rights also concern the relation between the state and the individual citizen. The citizen has rights, but on certain conditions. The concept of 'vertical relations' has been used to refer to the relationship between citizen and state as opposed to 'horizontal' mutual relations existing between the people. Thus a significant feature of the Western state model is a direct relation between the individuals and the state which over time has increasingly

Rie Odgaard, Anthropologist and Project Senior Researcher, Centre for Development Research, Copenhagen; Agnete Weis Bentzon, Professor Emeritus, Sociology of Law, University of Roskilde; she is currently affiliated to the Institute of Legal Science, University of Copenhagen.

replaced or supplemented peoples' rights and duties towards each other [*Eriksson, 1995*]. The most obvious examples of this trend are found in the area of social welfare regulation and legal proceedings. Personal concern for one's neighbour is to a great extent replaced by the payment of tax, and private punishment of offenses is made unlawful.

PIECEMEAL DEVELOPMENT OF LAW VERSUS THE COLONISERS' EXPORT OF LAW

Contemporary Western rules of law have a long piecemeal genesis. In early pre-Christian times, for example, among Germanic peoples, the clan and the family were the important social institutions which took care of the needs of their people and claimed their loyal co-operation. They carried out a number of functions which the nation state in the North fulfils for the population today.

Development of Family Law in the North

The development of legislation on family and succession in the North shows a transition from a legal system which protects the interests of the group, the clan, to a legal system which protects the interests of the individual. This process can be illustrated by the development of family law in Europe, and is, as we shall see, very important for understanding the development of legal systems in countries previously colonised by European countries.

The shift from legal concern with the extended family to that of the nuclear family and later to forms of cohabitation can be illustrated by short excerpts from Danish textbooks on family law. In a textbook from 1860 the 'family' includes all people living in the extended household [*Scheel, 1860: 706*]. But in the 1877 edition housemaids and farm hands are excluded from the concept of family because it is said 'they have lost their character of family' [*Scheel, 1877: foreword*].

The family law textbook of 1924 states that:

> family law includes the relations between the spouses and between parents and their children ... [I]n older times the concept of family included more people. The relatives had more legal and social importance. The family was often an extended family. The family included housemaids and siblings, who stayed in and were cared for by the household. The family was a closed economic unit [*Bentzon 1924: 8*].

About the contemporary situation in 1924 it is said:

> family relations do not bring about rights proper for the individual. The focus is on the duty to use rights for the benefit of the family. The rights

are given to make possible the fulfilment of the duties and obligations [*Bentzon 1924: 8*].

Finally, a textbook from 1991, which is still in use, has sections on marriage, children, cohabitation and registered partnership. This mentions that equality between men and women and the integrity of the individual is sought and secured by legislation [*Taksøe-Jensen, 1991: 72*].

A doctoral thesis from 1993 sums up the situation in the field of family property law in the North as follows:

> Seen in a historical perspective the elements of the law of family property have changed significantly since its inception. In the community of property the essential transformation has been pluralism, fragmentation and primacy of the individual, which have brought about a marked distillation of the family principle; the development now tends towards 'a sum of individual rights'. Moreover a great deal of the basic social and ideological reasons for community rules have been eliminated [*Nielsen, 1993: 497*, English summary].

There seems to be a connection between a society's view of property rights and the predominant family form. Where the extended family is the prevailing family form, the idea of individual property rights is not prevalent. On the contrary, this idea seems to be closely connected to the nuclear family. Many contemporary societies, especially in developing countries, include a mixture of family forms but, as will be seen from our examples, whereas in Europe the change from extended family to nuclear family was accompanied by a change from group ownership to individual private property rights, the situation in former colonies is much more fluid.

Customary Law and European Law in Colonised Societies

As a result of colonialism European legal ideas and principles have been diffused throughout the world. In post-colonial African states, legal systems combine rules transferred from European legislation and common law and customary law as interpreted by the courts. The colonial powers exported their legal systems to countries with a fundamentally different nature and culture, and this has been problematic.

The nature of customary living law[1] in Greenland and in the majority of rural African societies is different from the nature of the legal systems imposed on these societies by the colonial powers, and has more in common with living law among the old Germanic families. Despite the fact that a welfare system has been developed in Greenland (which is still part of the Danish realm, but with its own home-rule system), the family continues to be a very important social institution. Likewise, for many rural Africans the family and the clan are still coherent groups which generate and uphold their own rules. Group members' interests are attended to by the group and mutual support is expected. Expectations of support and of help in solving conflicts are not directed towards the state. However, local entities are not untouched by the colonial past or by the post-colonial governments' political enterprises and the resulting changes in the economy. There is wide scope for choice, and for manipulation, between the various parts of the plural legal systems in African societies. Thus, some people may pursue their interests on some occasions by resorting to state authorities whilst on others they follow local norms. Or they may try to promote their individual interests by combining the two systems.

Where the colonial masters left legal regulation in certain areas to the indigenous population, they gave rise to the coexistence of a plurality of normative systems. Newly independent states strove to establish unification of law, generally by introducing a single, hierarchical system of courts for the whole country, although still with an obligation to take customary law into account in some fields. Whilst, in colonial times the choice of substantive law to be applied in a particular case in colonial times rested on an ethnic criterion, the so-called 'mode of life' criterion is now preferred. The 'mode of life'-criterion is used to differentiate parties who live mainly in accordance with customary law from those who do not. However, in most fields of law, the formal legal system is generally valid. It consists of Western legal systems introduced in the colonial era, new legislation introduced after independence, and common law precedents and local court precedents.

However, one thing is the general validity of the formal legal system in the courts, another is the extent to which the formal legal system is seen as legitimate by local authorities and people in their day-to-day administration of justice. Our Tanzanian example below illustrates that local people as well as local officials and indigenous authorities may choose not to use the legal court system and instead refer the case to customary living law in its ethnic context.

Two Models for Legal Decision-Making

Customary law includes substantive law and procedural law. Studies of conflict resolution in societies governed by customary law show that the model adopted is different from the model taught at Western law schools. The former is forward-looking and concerned with the consequences of decisions. It is also named the 'peace model' as the aim is to re-establish peace and preserve a functionally efficient community. The needs and resources of the parties to the dispute are considered, but the decisions are taken in the interest of the whole, and a person's social worth for the community is an important factor. By contrast, the lawyers' model is retrospective and rule-oriented. This law and order, or 'conformity model'. classifies the evidence according to established rules, and the decision, the legal consequence, is reached within the limits set by these rules. The responsibility for the decision does not rest with the legal decision maker in person. This is particularly the case when the rules give detailed instructions with respect to the rights and duties of the parties. In this case, the judge merely registers the legal situation.

The peace model has some societal preconditions: relatively isolated settlements where everybody knows each other, and where there is a need and use for all resources. The conformity model's preconditions are a differentiated, mobile and anonymous society, where cohesion is reduced by conflicting interests.

THE INDIVIDUAL AND THE COMMUNITY: RIGHTS AND OBLIGATIONS

The following examples illustrate some problems arising from the conflict between imported principles of law which mainly support the rights of the individual and local principles of law developed in a totally different societal context. The two societies we discuss have both been affected by colonialism and its accompanying Western legal ideology. Although different empirically and in nature, both examples illustrate the importance of seeing 'law' in its social context, and not only as an independent set of universal rules and principles.

The first example concerns a concrete homicide case among immigrant pastoral Maasai in south-western Tanzania; the second concerns a breach of local norms of solidarity in a small Greenlandic community of hunters of sea mammals.

Case 1: The Collective Resolution of a Crime

The incident occurred on a dark tropical night some years ago in a small village in Usangu Plains in the south Western Highlands of Tanzania. The village is located in an area which used to be sparsely populated but which, over the past few decades, has received a large number of immigrants – cultivators, pastoralists and agro-pastoralists – from different parts of Tanzania. The population of the village is thus ethnically very mixed [*Odgaard, 1987; 1994*]. Maasai pastoralists from Northern and Central Tanzania are among those who began migrating to Usangu in the mid-1950s.

On the night in question two Maasai youngsters were on their way home to a Maasai settlement situated in the 'bush' some kilometres from the village. To cut their journey short, they followed a footpath along one of the big irrigation canals on a nearby rice farm. There had been *Mnada* (a cattle market) that day, an event which always attracts large numbers of cattle herders from the many different cattle herding groups living in the area. The two young men had been drinking heavily in one of the bars in the village since market ended at sunset.

They were drunk and started arguing on their way home. The argument developed into a fight during which one received a blow which made him stumble,
fall into the irrigation canal and drown.

The next morning the matter was reported to the village chairman in the
village centre. From then on relations between the offender's family and the
family of the deceased would be strained until the matter was resolved. In
accordance with normal procedure in this part of Usangu, the 'kin-groups' of
the youngsters had two options for resolving the matter. The case could either
be seen as a homicide case, thereby involving the police and the court system
(the 'modern' way), or the two families could involve the customary
authorities and abide by the customary laws on manslaughter.

In general, villagers as well as local officials in this part of Tanzania prefer
to solve such problems through local customary mechanisms. Such
mechanisms exist at village level, and even at sub-village level, in the form of
Baraza la Wazee (a Council of Elders), and are recognised as part of the local
informal institutional set-up for conflict resolution in Tanzania [*Boesen,
Maganga and Odgaard, 1996*].[2] The criteria for being appointed to such
councils (whether council members should be ethnically mixed) vary and such
questions as length of office and extent of jurisdiction of the councils are
interpreted differently from one village to the other. In the village in question,
a *Baraza la Wazee* was composed of people who, in the eyes of the involved
parties and of local officials, were specially capable of solving the problem.

Given the possibility of choice between different semi-autonomous social
fields [*Moore, 1978*], the Maasai parties involved in the case opted to settle the
matter through their own customary mechanisms. In this particular case,
Maasai customary law was an obvious choice as the case concerned two
parties with the same ethnic background, and because of the existence of
extenuating circumstances in which the offender, it seemed, did not
deliberately kill the other person.

According to what appears to be the Maasai way of solving such problems
in Usangu at the present time,[3] the victim's family has a right to compensation,
usually in the form of cattle, for the loss suffered. The number of cattle to be
'paid' depends on the gravity of the offence. Once compensation is paid the
problem is normally considered solved, and the two families can go back to
'normal'.

To settle the matter the Maasai elders called a big meeting at which the
relatives of the two parties were present. The meeting lasted for several hours,
but no final solution was found. The defendant was ordered to pay a certain
number of cattle as compensation, but he did not himself possess enough cattle
to do so. Family members and relatives of the defendant were unwilling to pay
compensation on his behalf, although he would normally be entitled to such
help from relatives. They refused on the grounds that the defendant used to

have a lot of cattle, many of which he had inherited from his father, but he had lost almost all these by spending his money on alcohol and on dubious businesses.

His relatives expressed general dissatisfaction with his behaviour: he had been selfish. He had on occasion refused to help his closest family even though he was obliged to do so. His family found him unworthy of the help he would normally be entitled to under the Maasai system: he had not adhered to the proper Maasai behaviour of respecting the community. He had shown individualistic behaviour, managing family property as if it was his own private property.

Given this, there was no other solution than to hand over the defendant to the police and subject him to the 'modern' type of trial and punishment. In the case of manslaughter, this usually means imprisonment, especially as in this case he was not able to pay fines or bribes. The man was now considered an unfree man. His hands were tied with a rope in readiness to be handed over to the police. However, as the only means of transportation available was our vehicle we were asked if we could transport the defendant, the Maasai elders and the village chairman to the village. This was a precarious situation for us and, after agreeing, we dropped the party off a short distance from the police officer's house.

The following day we were surprised to learn that the defendant was never handed over to the police. The walk to the police officer's house had provided a chance to talk the matter over a second time. At the last minute, the defendant's relatives promised to pay compensation on the condition that he changed his behaviour. Should he fail to do so, he would be subjected to sanctions.

The reasoning behind this solution was the following. If the defendant was handed over to the police, nobody would benefit from the situation, on the contrary all parties stood to lose. The relatives of the deceased would not receive any compensation, and the relatives of the defendant would not be able to live in peace with their neighbours. Moreover, while in prison the defendant would not be able to work or take care of his family; a situation which might involve expenses for the relatives. Furthermore, imprisonment and a possible court case might involve the defendant's relatives in additional expenses, whether they liked it or not.

This example shows how the general formal legal system is inappropriate for solving conflicts between parties who in principle agree that conflict resolution should maintain or restore peace between the families. In this case the conflict is regarded as a family concern, involving the offender's family and the victim's family. However, the general legal system sees the conflict as between the individual offender and the state. The victim and the respective families are outsiders who are not allowed, in principle, to seek revenge themselves. The state insists on a monopoly with respect to reprisals. Where a choice of forum for settling conflicts exists, a preference may be expressed for the official legal system in cases where the offender has not earned the loyalty and solidarity of his family and community.[4] On the other hand, the existence of the official legal system serve as an inducement for people to comply with customary principles of law.

Case 2: A Breach of Local Solidarity Norms

In the 1940s in the small settlements of Northern Greenland hunting of sea mammals by kayak was the dominant trade. In colonial Greenland the local council in the settlements consisted of Greenlanders only, and was the lowest level in the administrative hierarchy. It also had some judicial powers.

A hunter from southern Greenland, who owned a motor boat, took up residence in one such settlement. He soon came into conflict with the local population because he did not follow the local custom of sharing the bag of sea mammals, according to a set pattern, with the rest of the settlement. Instead, he kept part of the bag for himself and sold the rest to the Royal Greenlandic Trade Company to pay off the instalments on his new motor boat. He kept his contract with the Royal Greenland Trade Company to avoid running the risk of losing his boat. He was the sole owner of a motorboat, and the other hunters held that the sound of the motor scared off the sea mammals and reduced their bag. An additional source of discontent related to the size of his bag, which was much bigger than that of the kayak hunters, largely because the technically more advanced boat made it possible for him to employ a different hunting pattern. They also argued that this hunting pattern (which involved sailing farther out into the open sea than the kayak hunters) had a negative impact on their chances of a good bag.

One winter night, after a birthday party, the motor boat owner was assaulted by three hunters, and left unconscious in the snow. He was found by others and survived. The three attackers were ordered by the local council to pay a considerable fine. However, when interviewed some years later, the chairman of the council disclosed that the fines were never recovered. The reason why this matter was not pursued was that it might have angered the attackers and led them to move to another settlement. By this time the motor boat owner had left the settlement.[5]

This example demonstrates that the violent reaction of the local population to a breach of local solidarity norms was condoned by the local authority, even though the colonial power had vested the council with the power to punish people for taking the law into their own hands. Obviously the norms stemming from the immediate entourage carried more weight with council members than the norms of a distant central government. Respect for local norms is a precondition for preserving peace in the community. The example also underlines that protection of collective interests entails no, or very little, protection of individuals with low social esteem in the community.

CONCLUSION

The focus of this contribution has been on the interplay between collective rights and obligations and individual rights in countries with plural legal systems. The two illustrative cases from North and South are from small local societies in a process of change, sometimes labelled modernisation. This type of society is dominated by a subsistence economy controlled by clans, households and families with collective rights and obligations. The members of the community are both taken care of and controlled by the community. Any breach of collective law is punished and there is very limited individual protection. The nation state is weak or almost non-existent.

However, these societies are undergoing fundamental change: development of a market economy, industrialisation of production and an emerging regulation of inter-individual relations by the nation state and protection of the individual against self-help justice. New customs and values have been introduced alongside, and sometimes in competition with, earlier customs and value orientations. As illustrated by our cases, collective rights and obligations are confronted with the rights of the individual in such processes of transition.

Where the nation state has been able to enforce state law, it has sometimes led to solutions which are considered unjust by the local population. Where the state has introduced individual rights, without providing the services and fulfilling the obligations once secured by collective rights and obligations, the result has been disaster for some.

As far as governments are concerned, the situation calls for the harmonisation of the rules of the formal law system with the local norms followed by different groups of the population. For the law reformer, therefore, this means being familiar with the existing living law as well as the formal law. However, harmonisation should not be understood as incorporating living law into formal law. This would result in living law becoming rigid and unresponsive to changes in society. By harmonisation we mean the following: the state vests local leaders, who enjoy legitimacy in the eyes of the local people, with the power to decide which rules and norms to apply in particular cases coming before the local justice system. Local authorities know living customary law and follow its ever changing rules and norms. Thus these countries should not attempt to follow a Western path with respect to the relationship between law and society, nor return to the pre-colonial situation, but to find a third alternative.

Post-colonial history in Tanzania shows that this has not always been accomplished or even taken into account. However, recent developments indicate that a move towards 'the third direction' may be under way. The presidential commission which forms part of an investigation into the land question in Tanzania, and which preceded present efforts to pass a new land act[6] is, we think, an example of official recognition of the importance of both living law and formal law in relation to law reform.[7]

The need for structures which can facilitate a 'dialogue' between living law and formal law is, in our opinion, also recognised in Tanzania. The existence of the informal *Baraza la Wazee* (council of elders) for resolving conflicts at the village level is an indication of this as is the incorporation of the *Baraza la Usuluhishi* (conflict resolution council) institution in the formal legal set-up at Ward level.

In Greenland the Greenland Law Reform Committee was established in 1951 with the aim of preparing a draft bill of common laws for Greenlanders and Danes in Greenland. Danish legislation was taken as its starting point but respect was to be had for Greenlandic customs and conditions. Law reforms were but one part of a larger catalogue of reforms which were effected as part of the decolonisation process after the Second World War. This meant changes in all areas of life in Greenland.

The necessary respect for customs and conditions could only be taken seriously by continuously adapting legislation on the basis of knowledge of living customary law. To this end, the law committee cooperated with the committee for social research in Greenland.

Finally, a common element in the two cases merits a comment. A system of economic competition, which existed both in the Greenlandic and the Tanzanian examples, does not in itself violate the rights of the community. But if the prosperous person individually keeps the profits, and the state is not ready to take up the obligations he neglects towards members of his community, he may be excluded one way or the other.

It is worth noting that the welfare states of the North is now tending to draw on the kind of resources which exist or are presumed to exist in the form of solidarity between people in the workplace and in the family. Employers and fellow workers are, for example, expected to show consideration for women with infants, and the social welfare administration increasingly expects family members to take care of their old people, even if they do not share the same household. This indicates that there is little support for a theory of linear development of law and society.

NOTES

1. The term 'living law' was coined by Eugen Ehrlich [*1936*] to refer to those customs and norms which rule behaviour in everyday life and guide the resolution of informal conflicts. Living laws are rules *of* conduct. State laws are rules *for* conduct. Whether they are followed is an empirical question.

2. The important role played by councils of elders in conflict resolution in Africa is not new. In the case of the Maasai, this institution has always been part and parcel of their indigenous legal structure, although it has constantly changed in form and sphere of jurisdiction as a result of interaction with external systems. Conflict resolution councils (in Swahili: *Baraza la Usuluhishi*) are now part of the formal legal set-up at Ward level in Tanzania. Such councils also previously existed informally at the village level. Where the *Baraza la Wazee* at village level are unable to resolve a case, it is referred to *Baraza la Usuluhishi* at ward level [*Boesen, Maganga and Odgaard 1996*].

3. Systems are constantly changing so current rules and norms in Usangu do not necessarily correspond to rules and norms in other places where the Maasai live, or to rules and norms previously in use in the home area of the Maasai.

4. Niels Christie [*1977*] discusses the problems relating to victim(s), and his observations are relevant for both the Tanzanian and Greenland case presented here. His point is that hardly any attention is paid to the victim or rather the victims in any particular case. (In most cases there are losses on both sides implying that people other than those directly involved in a dispute are affected). However, not even the immediate victim is drawn into the actual criminal case. A claim for compensation by the victim can be included in the criminal case, but the police usually refer the victim to a private lawsuit. The defendant is normally unable to pay compensation to the victim, whether he is jailed or fined. The fine is paid to the Treasury and is recovered in advance of a claim for damages.

5. The interview was conducted by members of the juridical expedition to Greenland 1948-49 and their Greenlandic interpreter. See Bentzon, Goldschmidt and Lindegaard [*1950*].

6. We are referring here to the presidential commission set up to inquire into formal as well as living laws pertaining to land rights and land tenure in Tanzania. A summary of its results is published in: Report of the Presidential Commission of Inquiry into Land Matters, Vol.1: Land Policy and Land Tenure Structure [*Presidential Commission of Inquiry into Land Matters, 1994*].

7. To what extent this will be reflected in the final version of the new land act in Tanzania is yet to be seen. As far as we are aware, the land act has not yet been passed (May 1998).

REFERENCES

Bentzon, A.W., 1968, *Familiens økonomiske administration og ejendelenes tilhørsforhold i de vestgrønlandske samfund* (The Organisation of the Family and the Ownership of Items of Property in West Greenlandic Societies), Copenhagen: New Social Science Monographs.

Bentzon, Viggo, 1924, *Familieretten* (Family Law), Copenhagen: Gad.

Bentzon, A.W., Goldschmidt, V. and P. Lindegaard, 1950, 'Betænkning fra Den Juridiske Ekspedition til Grøland Bind 1–5' (Report of the Juridical Expetition and Its Fieldwork in Greenland), mimeo, Copenhagen.

Boesen, J., Maganga, F. and R. Odgaard, 1996, unpublished fieldnotes.

Bottomley S., Gunningham, N. and S. Parker (eds.), 1994, *Law in Context*, Annandale: The Federation Press.

Christie, Niels, 1977, 'Konflikt som ejendom' (Conflict as Property), *Tidskrift for Retsvidenskab.* Vol.51.

Ehrlich, Eugen, 1936, *Fundamental Principles of the Sociology of Law*, New York: Arno Press (1975 edition).

Eriksson, L.D., 1995, 'Ansvarsetik eller rättighetsmoral?' (Ethics of Responsibility or Morality of rights), *Retfærd*, Vol.18, No.69, pp.3–13.

Moore, Sally Falk, 1978, *Law as Process*, London: Routledge & Kegan Paul.

Nielsen, Linda, 1993, 'The Law of Family Property in a Changing Society', *Familieformueretten*, (Family property law), pp.497–502.

Odgaard, Rie, 1987, 'De tog til Usangu! -Bondemigration i det Sydvestlige højland, Tanzania' (They went to Usangu! – Peasant Migration in the South Western Highland, Tanzania), *Den Ny Verden* (The New World), Vol.20, No.3, pp.69–91.

Odgaard, Rie, 1994, 'Jordbesiddelsesformer og bæredygtig ressourceudnyttelse – eksemplet Tanzania' (Forms of Land Tenure and Sustainable Resource Utilization – The Example of Tanzania), *Den Ny Verden* (The New World), Vol.27, No.2, pp.50–68.

Presidential Commission of Inquiry into Land Matters, 1994, *Report of the Presidential Commission of Inquiry into Land Matters, Vol.1: Land Policy and Land Tenure Structure*, Uppsala: Scandinavian Institute of African Studies.

Scheel, A. W., 1860, *Familieret* (Family Law), Copenhagen: Gyldendal.

Scheel, A. W., 1877, *Familieret* (Family Law) (Second Edition), Copenhagen: Gyldendal.

South African Law Commission, 1997, 'Project 90: The Harmonisation of the Common Law and the Indigenous Law', *Discussion Paper No.74* (Customary Marriages), Pretoria.

Taksøe-Jensen, F., 1991, *Person-, Familie-, Arve- og Skifteret* (Person, Family, Inheritance and Estate Law), Copenhagen: Gad.

Governance as Multilateral Development Bank Policy: The Cases of the African Development Bank and the Asian Development Bank

MORTEN BØÅS

The problem for the Banks in question is that an issue like governance can easily boil down to questions of individual political rights, whilst their charters exclude concepts like civil rights from loan considerations. The dilemma the Banks face is that donor countries insist on incorporation of good governance into Bank policy, while recipient countries fear that policies on governance may infringe on their national sovereignty. The argument put forward here is that if a governance policy is to be more than just lip-service, these Banks must walk the narrow path between consensus and controversy. They must avoid an explicit focus on individual political rights, but their governance policies must have a broader focus than collective economic rights. They must have a particular focus on institutional and political interaction within the public realm.

INTRODUCTION

In the African Development Bank (AfDB) and the Asian Development Bank (ADB), governance has recently emerged as an important issue-area. On 3 October 1995, the ADB became the first Multilateral Development Bank (MDB) to establish a Board-approved policy on governance. In its African counterpart – the AfDB – governance as an issue-area emerged in discussions on reorganisation of the Bank in 1996. Governance is the most recent issue-area on these institutions' agenda, but it has generated a great deal of controversy and debate in the short time it has been around. The main reason is that recipient member states fear that Bank policies on governance may infringe their national sovereignty and further politicise decisions on their loans. However, these countries are not the only ones to have problems with governance. This is also a difficult concept for the MDBs who do not want to

Morten Bøås, Research Fellow, Centre for Development and Environment, University of Oslo, Norway.

be seen as political and have since their establishment advocated the doctrine
of political neutrality. They have embraced the functionalist logic that
technical and economic questions can be separated from politics. For instance,
in the *Agreement Establishing the African Development Bank* and the
Agreement Establishing the Asian Development Bank the following principle
of political neutrality is stated.

> The Bank, its President, vice-presidents, officers and staff shall not
> interfere in the political affairs of any members; nor shall they be
> influenced in their decisions by the political character of the member
> concerned. Only economic considerations shall be relevant to their
> decisions. Such considerations shall be weighed impartially in order to
> achieve and carry out the functions of the Bank [*AfDB, 1964: Art. 38;
> ADB, 1982: Art. 36*].

The problem for the AfDB and the ADB is that cross-cutting issues like
governance are easily reduced to questions concerned with individual political
rights. In fact, the Banks' charters exclude concepts like civil rights and
democracy from loan considerations. The dilemma the Banks face is that
donor countries insist on incorporation of the governance nexus into Bank
policy. Subsequently, the Banks' main problem is that the accommodation of
conflicting and diverse issues like governance into co-operative action is a
political question, and if these Banks are to become involved in such activities
they will have to interfere in the political affairs of their member countries,
basing their decisions to some extent on the political character of member
countries.

The argument put forward here is that if a governance policy is to be more
than just cosmetic, the Banks must walk a tightrope between consensus and
controversy. The first step in the argument presents some thoughts on the
interaction between the issue-area of governance and the state–civil society
relationship. The next step addresses the governance debate in the two Banks.
Finally, the implications for state–civil society relations in recipient member
countries in Africa and Asia is discussed.

This article concerns two MDBs, the AfDB and the ADB, but no attempt
is made to undertake a formal comparative analysis. The aim is merely to offer
an interpretation of why governance is on the agenda of these institutions, how
they have approached this issue-area, and what kind of implications their
approaches have for state–civil society relations in their borrowing member
countries. From this analysis, some preliminary conclusions on governance are
drawn in an attempt to suggest a way ahead.

(GOOD) GOVERNANCE AND THE STATE–CIVIL SOCIETY NEXUS

According to the Commission on Global Governance, governance is the sum of the ways in which individuals and institutions, in public and private spheres, manage their common affairs in order to accommodate diverse and conflictual views. However, prior to the spotlight on governance on the international agenda it was present in more narrow political (academic) discourses as a generic concept, referring to the task of running a government, or any other public or private organisation [*Hyden, 1992*]. More or less at the same time as the launch of the Stockholm Initiative,[1] the World Bank started to employ the concept, identifying the African crisis as one of a crisis of governance. More precisely, the World Bank operationalised 'bad' governance as personalisation of power, lack of human rights, endemic corruption and un-elected and unaccountable governments [*World Bank, 1989; 1991; 1992*].

If such situations can be defined as a crisis of governance, that is, bad governance, then good governance must be the natural opposite. The call for good governance from bilateral and multilateral donors today is therefore, at least implicitly, a call for political and economic liberalisation, democratisation, accountability and respect for basic individual human rights. It is an attempt to promote individual political rights. Accordingly, the issue of (good) governance is interwoven with and embedded in state–civil society relationships.

With respect to civil society, experience suggests a wide range of alternatives which are partly overlapping but not necessarily mutually exclusive. They range from popular participation and bargaining among the elite to interaction between citizens and the government. Nevertheless, the main assumption in the literature is civil society's ability to establish pathways between society and government. Civil society can therefore be seen as:

(1) buffer against government and society, (2) broker between government and society, (3) symbol of actual political norm setter, (4) agent of change, (5) regulator of the process of participation in societal norm setting, (6) integrator of groups articulating political interests into a viable process for doing so, (7) representative of particular interests, and (8) midwife of regime change [*Harbeson, 1994: 22*].

Different as these various interpretations of civil society may be, the element which unites them is an understanding of the relationship between state and civil society as one of reciprocity. In other words, if we were to ask what constitutes civil society it cannot be answered without an understanding of the nature of the state in question and *vice versa*. If the state and civil society are constituted through iterated interaction, the issue of governance (bad or good) is also an outcome of the same process. However, governance should not be seen as just another equivalent to the state–civil society problematic, but as an aspect of the public realm that encompasses both. The demarcation line is thus between private and public. The governance nexus has to do with whether there exists a civic public realm, how it is maintained by political actors both in state and society, and whether access to participation in the public realm is built on respected and legitimate rules.

As such, governance is concerned with the regime which constitutes the set of fundamental rules for the organisation of the public realm, and not with government. Both governance and government refer to goal-oriented activities and systems of rule, but whereas government suggests constituted policies backed by formal authority, governance refers to activities backed by shared goals that may or may not derive from legal and formal authority [*Rosenau, 1992*]. Governance clearly embraces governmental institutions, but it also subsumes informal, non-governmental institutions operating within the public realm.

As a system of rule, governance is therefore as dependent on inter-subjective meanings as on formally sanctioned constitutions and charters: it will only work if it is accepted by the majority (or at least by the most powerful actors within the system). Subsequently, governance is equivalent to the management of regime structures for the purpose of enhancing the legitimacy of the public realm. Good governance creates legitimacy together with the social capital that keeps people motivated and results in their contribution to public causes. Thus, governance and actual policy-making are both separated and interwoven entities. Good governance, not only ensures the legitimacy of the regime which governs the public realm, it also confers legitimacy on the actual decision-makers.

To sum up, governance, both in the broad sense (as the sum of the ways in which individuals and institutions, public and private, manage their common affairs) and in the more narrow understanding (as the maintenance of the regime structure which supervises the public realm) is embedded in and interwoven with state–civil society interaction in any given nation. The recent MDB emphasis on the governance issue therefore highlights MDBs' role as political actors and increases the concern of member states about infringements of their national sovereignty. Recipient member countries fear that increased importance of governance issues will entail an emphasis on individual political rights in loan considerations.

GOVERNANCE AND THE AFRICAN DEVELOPMENT BANK

Some believe that because the AfDB is a MDB controlled by African countries themselves, it is in a privileged position to address the so-called governance crisis on the African continent compared to the World Bank and

other multilateral and bilateral donors [*Peprah, 1994: 129–30*]. The argument
is that the AfDB should be able to discuss the issue of governance with
African countries in a less suspicious atmosphere than that surrounding extra-
regional organisations. However, the counter argument can be made that
because the Bank is controlled by the African countries themselves, it is too
close to the governance problem in Africa to be willing and/or able to get
involved in it.

The main problem for the institution, however, is that the charter of the
AfDB, like that of most other MDBs,[2] discourages the Bank from emphasising
political considerations like civil rights and democracy in its lending decisions.
Moreover, because the AfDB is formally controlled by the African member
countries, it is more responsive to the will of its borrowing member countries
than other MDBs. With both the presidency and vice-presidencies determined
by the institution's borrowing member countries, the Bank's top management
is quite naturally reluctant to push too hard on the governance issue. The space
available for entrepreneurial manoeuvring and expressions of firm leadership
by the AfDB within this issue area is therefore quite limited. Nevertheless, the
extra-regional donor countries, which the Bank depends on for capital increase
and replenishment, now demand action by the Bank on this issue.
Subsequently, the AfDB has had to tread the thin dividing line between
governance/donors and accusations of political interference/borrowers.

In policy papers and approaches, the Bank has taken some small steps to
carve out a niche for itself. The Bank's poverty alleviation strategy has
promised changes in the approach in order to incorporate governance issues.
The attention is now on participatory approaches to development, a greater
role for women and improved co-operation with NGOs [*AfDB, 1992*].
However, vague statements like these do not impress anybody these days, and
most observers seem to agree that the Bank's actual track record of
implementation of these vague statements has not been very impressive [*Bøås,
1996; English and Mule, 1996*].

In an attempt to remove the governance issue from the blind alley in which
it seemed stuck, the Bank's African Advisory Council submitted a report to the
Bank in 1994 on the theme *democratisation processes and governance*.[3] The
advisory council's main argument was that:

> The success of the development enterprise itself is dependent on the
> consolidation of democracy, as well as on the existence of good
> governance. The Bank, although primarily a financial institution, has, of
> necessity, to be involved in these two sets of issues [*AfDB, 1994a: 1*].

In the report, a wide range of recommendations for Bank involvement in the
promotion of democracy was put forward. For example, employment
generation, poverty alleviation, education, the private sector, political and

economic integration, the establishment of an endogenous science and technology base and research. Moreover, in order to facilitate good governance, the report argued the need for more comprehensive policy advice to regional members, and projects and programmes which address these issues in a more integrated and direct manner than the traditional adjustment programmes of the Bank. According to the Council, the AfDB's adjustment, research and training policies should be brought in line with African norms and values. The Bank should develop an African approach to governance. However, when it comes to identifying what an African approach to governance should be, the report is unclear. Apart from the rejection of the idea of negative conditionalities as a way of promoting policy objectives, and opting instead for the provision of additional resources to the well-doers, the report fails to come up with any suggestions which can be operationalised.[4]

The question was what the Bank was supposed to do, squeezed as it was between donors (with badly needed fresh cash) and borrowers (with voting power). The answer came with the report from a Task Force on Project Quality (the Knox report) which was submitted to the Bank's Board and its Governors.[5] The Knox report described the Bank as a chaotic top-heavy bureaucracy, weakened by the impoverishment of the continent it was meant to help, and full of political intrigue and suspicion. The report argued that if the Bank was not significantly reformed, the institution might end up destroying itself. Moreover, the Task Force found that the Bank was being pulled in all directions – staff and management mistrusted the Board and *vice versa* – and the presidency, although formally vested with authority, had little power compared to (some of) the 18-member Board of Directors. The Bank's personnel had been unable to keep up with the pace of growth in project lending and scant attention was paid to the quality of loans as opposed to volume. Thus armed, leading non-regional member countries demanded fundamental changes before they would consider replenishing the soft window of the AfDB, the African Development Fund.

Just after the conclusions of the Knox report had hit the Bank headquarters in Abidjan in April 1994, discussions on what to do with the Bank's former focal forum for cross-cutting issues, the Social and Environment Policy Division, started. Several suggestions were put forward. The division itself argued strongly that it should be turned into a department directly under one of the vice-presidents, whereas others argued for streamlining the Bank's expertise on cross-cutting issues into the country programming departments. Internal discussions on this issue went back and forth for a substantial period of time. In fact, no progress had been made on governance or on placing the other cross-cutting issues within the organisational framework of the Bank before an internal task force/working group was established in March 1996.

I would propose that a working group or a special task force be set up immediately with staff experts in these areas and responsible people at different levels, which should be asked to review in more detail this unit's functional objectives and responsibilities and try to define its longer term resource needs based on the general policy directions we should expect to follow. It should also address all those cross-cutting themes that are relevant, including governance, population issues etc. [*AfDB, 1996a: 1*].[6]

This was in fact the first time governance was explicitly raised in the debate on a new focal point for cross-cutting issues in the AfDB. The next time, however, these questions were raised at a Board meeting on 19 February 1996 governance was substituted with NGO co-operation and institutional development. At this meeting it was decided that the most effective way of creating a focal point for such cross-cutting themes as poverty, women-in-development, environment, NGOs and institutional development in the Bank was to create a support function within the Operations vice-presidency.[7] The main objective of this Unit was supposedly to enhance the Bank's strategic direction and to ensure in an independent manner, the formulation and monitoring of Bank-wide policies and guidelines for environment and the classification of projects, environmental impact assessment and the social dimension of projects. The terms of reference for the unit and its staff requirements were left to the internal task force to figure out. Among other issues, the task force should therefore:

Assess the staff needs in the various disciplines based on the Bank's operational priorities and external recruitment in the areas of environment, women-in-development, social sector, private sector and governance [*AfDB, 1996b: 1*].

Governance was, therefore, mentioned as a separate issue-area in the terms of reference for the internal task force, but in the final report from the task force the term governance was substituted with institutional development. According to the report from the task force, which was approved by the Board in June 1996, a new Environment and Sustainable Development Unit (OESU) should be established.

The Environment and Sustainable Development Unit (OESU) – which comprises the cross-cutting issues of environment, gender, poverty reduction, population, NGOs and institutional development – develops and updates policies, guidelines; monitors their implementation; provides advice for designing and implementing country strategies and operational programmes; and participates – when necessary – as members of the project team in preparing, appraising, supervising and evaluating (post-mortem) projects. Through linking the concerns on social dimensions with environmental assessment, the Unit ensures a harmonious and long-term balancing of basic human needs and critical natural resources in the borrowing member countries [AfDB, 1996c: Annex IV].

The OESU is therefore supposed to serve as the Bank's focal point for reviewing environmental and social concerns and for the promotion of environmental and social awareness within the Bank and borrowing member countries. With respect to the Bank's governance substitute – institutional development – the OESU main policy functions are to:

(a) prepare the Bank's institutional development policy, and the procedures and guidelines necessary to assist staff to integrate this area into the project cycle;

(b) disseminate current developments within the field of institutional development, collect comparative data on this area in the Bank's borrowing member countries and prepare policy studies in the area;

(c) co-ordinate Bank participation in international and regional fora on institutional development, monitor Bank progress in integrating institutional development factors into Bank operations, and to design and assist in delivering training programmes on institutional development to staff and officials in borrowing member countries.

and the OESU main operational functions are to:

(a) ensure that Country Strategy Papers and policy dialogue with member countries reflect institutional strengthening activities;

(b) ensure provisions of direct support to institutional strengthening operations and participate, when found necessary, in different phases of the project cycle for all projects with institutional development components;

(c) report on how effectively the Bank has provided, and borrowers have used assistance for institutional building/strengthening.

In short, the new unit is supposed to be both the developer of new policies and the watchdog of the Bank's action on cross-cutting issues. Thus, the next question is what implications such an approach to governance will have for state–civil society relations in the AfDB's borrowing member countries. We will turn to this question after having looked at the governance debate in the Asian Development Bank.

GOVERNANCE AND THE ASIAN DEVELOPMENT BANK

On 10 February 1997, Shoji Nishimoto, Chief of the ADB's Strategy and Policy Office, cut the ribbon officially opening the Governance and Capacity Building Resource Room in the Bank's headquarters. The Governance and Capacity Building Resource Group (GCB-RG) is supposed to serve as the key unit for governance and capacity building within the institution. The tasks of GCB-RG include gathering, producing, and disseminating relevant information and approaches in the field of governance and public sector management in both the Asia and Pacific region, and throughout the globe. On request it is supposed to be able to provide support and advice to Bank programmes and projects departments working on governance and capacity building issues. Such assistance could include consultation and referrals on country strategy assistance programmes, loans, technical assistance, and providing hands-on support for selected projects, and training [ADB, 1997]. Finally, the group can recommend adjustments in ADB policies and procedures in order to make the Bank more effective in promoting governance and capacity building.

Currently, seven Bank staff and consultants are assigned to the GCB-RG, located by the Bank's Strategy and Policy Office. According to the plan, this small unit will serve as the core of a broader network of Bank staff working to make the provisions of the Bank's governance policy a reality. Whether it will succeed is still too early to say. Nevertheless, encouragingly, at least for the group position *vis-à-vis* other departments within the Bank, it has already managed to involve itself in issues ranging from municipal management in South Asian mega-cities to decentralisation of education services in Indonesia.

However, more interesting from the perspective of this article is the question of (1) what does the ADB actual mean by governance and capacity building, and (2) why has the Bank suddenly become so concerned about such a difficult issue-area for itself as governance?

The ADB acknowledges that governance is a multi-dimensional concept which means different things to different people [ADB, 1995a]. Nevertheless, among the many definitions of governance, the Bank chose the one from the 1979 edition of *Webster's New Universal Unabridged Dictionary* where governance is defined as 'the manner in which power is exercised in the management of a country's social and economic resources for development'. Likewise, capacity building is defined as, 'strengthening the national framework within a developing member country that affects the direction, management and sustenance of the development process in a sector and the economy as a whole' [ADB, 1997: 1].

The question is what this actually means? Are governance and capacity building just two sides of the same question or are they analytically and conceptually different, albeit inter-related? Is the ADB version of governance in line with the broad version (the sum of the ways in which individuals and institutions, private and public, manage their common affairs) or is the Bank's version more in line with the narrow understanding of governance as the maintenance of the regime structure which supervises the public realm. This is not an inherently difficult question, but for a regional political institution which prefers to be non-political it is a tricky one and one to which the ADB is unable to give a straightforward answer. In its latest publication on governance it is stated that:

> Although useful in framing the discussion, both definitions are too broad to give concrete operational guidance. Furthermore, the practical or analytical rationale for differentiating between them is often unclear. Since most of the Bank's work on governance is devoted to building the capacity of public sector institutions, Bank staff are encouraged to use the shorthand term 'Governance and Capacity Building' (or GCB) when referring to these issues [*ADB, 1997: 1*].

Taken word for word this quote only increases the confusion about the notion of governance in the ADB. Reading between the lines, however, an interesting story emerges about the Bank's preferred public image. This story is related to the second question, why did the Bank suddenly became so concerned about such a difficult issue-area?

Governance, like most other cross-cutting issues (indigenous people, involuntary resettlement, gender, environment and so on) which have played a prominent role in the recent international development debate, is a donor/NGO-driven issue. Quite often such issues have been forced down the throat of MDBs and developing member countries by donors who are suffering from donor-fatigue and facing NGOs lobbying for what they perceive as a more sustainable development practice in MDBs.

> Good governance, democratic development and human rights are controversial issues in the Asian region with governments apprehensive of their implications for development assistance. They have opposed the introduction of conditionalities attached to lending that are political in nature [*Kappagoda, 1995: 148–49*].

Borrowing member countries would like to see as few conditionalities attached to their loans as possible not only because they disagree with the idea of individual political rights underpinning the conditionalities (for instance, Indonesia), but also because conditionalities mean less room for manoeuvre in their national developmental processes.

The ADB's position is somewhat similar. A lot of people in the Bank, particularly in the Programme Departments, the Strategy Policy Office and in the Office of the Environment and Social Development, are undoubtedly concerned about these issues, but for the Project Departments and the Bank as a whole these issues are difficult. The main reason lies in the Bank's charter, namely Article 36 which states that economic issues alone should be taken into consideration. Thus, the main problem with the issue of governance for the ADB is that it puts the Bank on a collision course with its charter and its preferred image of political neutrality. Governance is, therefore, the type of issue that the Bank would prefer to keep at bay. Such a strategy was, however, not a viable one. The publication of the World Bank reports, defining the crisis on the African continent as one of governance (or rather as a lack of good governance) and the Report of the Commission on Global Governance [*1995*], led to increased concern about governance issues in the international development debate. In fact, the ADB admits that it was this debate which spilled over into parallel discussions on the objectives, priorities and approaches of the operational programmes of the Bank [*ADB, 1995b*].

Prior to the ADB's Annual Meeting in 1994 several donor countries started to question what a regional development bank should do when its region has become, at least, partly developed. The general feeling among several major donor countries was that, since many of the developing countries in Asia had growing resources themselves and access to private capital, a capital increase for the ADB could only be justified if a substantial shift in Bank policy from 'economic growth and co-operation' to 'social progress' was made [*Bøås, 1996*]. Subsequently, replenishment of the Asian Development Fund and general capital increase was linked to more emphasis in the Bank on social sector issues, such as reducing poverty and improving the environment. Instead of simply financing a road, the role of the ADB was to ensure that the road would particularly benefit poor communities or, for example, that the recipient government charged appropriate fees to traffic in order to limit environmental damage. Such a change of focus represented an identity crisis for an institution geared towards industry and infrastructure, but most sensitive of all was the demand that loans should be linked to good governance.

Mr Zhou Zhengqing, the senior Chinese official attending the ADB's 1994 Annual Meeting in Nice, clearly expressed China's opposition when he stated that China did not agree with the linkage between policy and capital. According to the Chinese position these were totally different issues. Mr Mar'ie Muhammad, Indonesia's finance minister, argued that it was impractical and unrealistic to try to lay down the same set of all-embracing policies for all member countries. Thailand and India also expressed concern about the link between capital increase and lending policy, and Mr Mohammed Saifur Rahman, finance minister of Bangladesh, said that a majority of the Bank's developing country members were against including governance in the Bank's agenda. US officials, on the other hand, argued that they expected

governance guidelines to be applied flexibly and pragmatically, and that the
ADB should still be able to respond to the disparate needs of borrowing
members. In response the ADB argued that, as a bank, it could only use the
term (good governance) in an economic context, not a political one. In short,
governance was placed on the ADB agenda, but its meaning and purpose were
not clear.

From the ADB's point of view two things were clear: whilst governance as
an issue-area for the Bank could not be avoided, governance as
democratisation, individual political rights and human rights had to be avoided
if the Bank was to remain within its charter. In order to find a way out of the
conflicting views and opinions, the Bank undertook a study of East Asian
development experiences examining three specific aspects of governance, all
of which were more concerned with collective economic rights than with
individual political rights:

(a) Bureaucratic capability for the implementation of policies,
    programmes and projects.

(b) The government/business interface for effective policy outcomes.

(c) The principle of shared growth, from which the whole population
    stood to benefit.

In April 1995, a workshop on Governance and Development brought
together development practitioners and scholars from six of the high-
performing economies of the region: Hong Kong, Indonesia, Japan, South
Korea, Singapore and Taiwan. Not surprisingly, the dialogue at the workshop
revealed considerable apprehension among borrowers that an ADB
governance policy would reflect donor preferences and experiences. It was
argued by the regional representatives that existing definitions of governance
such as the one advocated by the OECD reflected the experience and interests
of Western donors (individual political rights) without taking into account
important components of the Asian experience (collective economic rights)
[*Root, 1996*].[8] In order to avoid such a Western bias, it was argued that the
knowledge gained in the workshop should constitute an important part of the
framework for an ADB policy paper on governance.[9]

A Western bias was to be avoided and it was subsequently agreed that
governance should be defined in accordance with the *Webster's New Universal
Unabridged Dictionary*, as the manner in which power is exercised in the
management of a country's economic and social resources for development.
What made this definition so attractive for the Bank and its Asian member
countries was that it links governance directly to public and private
management of the development process, and to collective economic rights
rather than individual political rights. According to the Bank:

> It encompasses the functioning and capability of the public sector, as
> well as the rules and institutions that create the framework for the
> conduct of both public and private business, including accountability for
> economic and financial performance, and regulatory frameworks
> relating to companies, corporations and partnerships. In broad terms,
> then, governance is about the institutional environment in which citizens
> interact among themselves and with government agencies/officials
> [*ADB, 1995b: 1–2*].[10]

In the ADB understanding, governance focuses almost exclusively on effective
management. Governance is therefore not a question of choosing the 'right'
policy, but a question of implementation. It concerns the norms and standards
of behaviour which ensure that political leaders are able to deliver what they
have promised to their fellow countrymen. What is emphasised is therefore not
the outspoken political dimension of governance (democracy, individual
political rights and human rights) but the so-called economic dimension of
governance which interprets good governance as sound developmental
management and emphasises collective economic rights. Governance is, more
than anything else, a tool that can facilitate adequate returns and the efficacy
of the programmes and projects financed by the Bank.

IMPLICATIONS FOR STATE–CIVIL SOCIETY RELATIONS

According to the current dominant view, democracy and democratisation are
equal to good government on a global scale. Good governance is often seen as
going 'hand in glove' with individual political rights and democratisation. The
argument is that you cannot have one without the other. Good governance is
impossible without democracy and *vice versa*. This is, as we have seen, not the
AfDB/ADB approach to governance. For these institutions, governance is
institutional development and sound development management, respectively.
It is not necessarily linked to the issue of democracy and democratisation in
their borrowing member countries but to issues more concerned with
collective economic rights. The questions which arise, therefore, are first, what
is the difference, if any, between governance as institutional development and
governance as sound development management, and second, what
implications do these approaches to governance have for state–civil society
relations in the Banks' developing member countries?

We have already established that the issue of governance is embedded in
and interwoven with the state–civil society relationship. State and civil society
are constituted through iterated interaction, and the governance produced (bad
or good) is an outcome of this process. Governance is concerned with the set
of fundamental rules for the organisation of the public realm. If the Banks'

approaches and policies to governance are to pay more than lip-service to the international donor community, they must be able to address and influence the relationship between state and civil society within the public realm. How can governance as institutional development and governance as sound development management accomplish this task? Can approaches to governance, which exclude democratisation, democracy and individual political rights from the equation, affect state–civil society issues?

One could, of course, turn this question upside-down by asking whether it is appropriate for these institutions to formulate policies which will put them at loggerheads with their customers. There is without doubt a significant degree of Western bias in the international development dialogue, and it is not unthinkable that a more pragmatic approach may be better suited to the circumstances than the one advocated by Western donors.

> So far, most proselytising about governance takes places among international organisations dominated by the experience of the donor, most of whom are Western nations. Japan was the only Asian nation to participate in the pronouncement of the Development Assistance Committee of the Organisation for Economic Co-operation and Development [see OECD 1995]. In this document, no reference was made to the recent experience of contemporary Asia, but many statements elevated the Western path to be the universal prototype of development [*Root, 1996: 146*].

One obvious reason behind the AfDB's and the ADB's reluctance to address governance as political liberalisation and democratisation is that their charters clearly state that they should not invoke political considerations in their lending decisions. Nevertheless, we should not dismiss the possibility that governance as institution-building and governance as sound development management can constitute the first steps towards an African and Asian approach to governance.

From the perspective of the work-load and manpower devoted to governance in the two institutions, there is little doubt that governance as an issue area is more established in the ADB than in the AfDB. As we have seen, the ADB has formulated a Board-approved policy on governance, and a governance group (GCB-RG) has been established within the Strategy and Policy Office. In the AfDB no policy paper on governance has yet been written, and no staff member in OESU has special responsibility for governance as such.

Other differences can also be observed, such as the way in which governance as an issue-area has been incorporated into the organisational structure of the institution. In the ADB, governance is separated from other cross-cutting issues which are dealt with by the Office of the Environment and

Social Development and the Programme Departments, whereas in the AfDB governance is under the same roof as the other cross-cutting issues in the OESU. What implications do these differences have for state–civil society relations?

One point of departure is the working definition/operationalisation offered by the ADB, namely that, 'governance is about the institutional environment in which citizens interact among themselves and with government agencies/officials' [ADB, 1995b: 2]. This definition is not unlike the interpretation whereby governance is concerned with the operation of the public realm. If governance is connected in one way or another to the institutional environment in which citizens and government/state and society interact then governance is an issue of the public realm. It comprises questions of how it is maintained by political actors both in state and society and whether access to participation in the public realm is built on respected and legitimate rules.

In other words, governance as sound development management can have a significant effect on state–civil society relations without an explicit focus on democracy and democratisation. If one of the main tasks of civil society is to establish pathways between society and government, a governance policy which emphasises interaction in the public realm has the potential of increasing the role of civil society both as a buffer and broker between government and society; as a symbol of political norms, agent of change, regulator of participation and integrator of group interests; and as the representative of particular interests and a midwife of change [Harbeson, 1994: 22].

The potential is therefore present. It is not the presence of words like democratisation and democracy which determine whether the governance policy of the ADB is mere donor-driven lip-service or not, but the actual focus of the policy. It is too early to reach a verdict regarding the ADB's governance policy, but if one were to hazard a word of warning this would be on the separation of governance from the other cross-cutting issues in the institutional structure. If the Bank really intends to link its governance policy to interaction in the public realm in a manner which makes sense for other cross-cutting issues, the institution should pool these issues at the start of any project because it is cross-cutting issues, such as environment, indigenous people, involuntary resettlement and gender, which really need support from a governance policy focused on citizens-government interaction in the public realm.

In the AfDB governance is substituted for the term institutional development, and, as we have seen from the review of that Bank's work on governance, no actual policy and working definition has yet been produced. In this respect, the AfDB is clearly lagging behind its sister institution in Asia.

However, we may look at the issue from another angle. In contrast to the situation in ADB, governance/institutional development is treated as a cross-cutting issue and pooled with other cross-cutting issues in the OESU. The advantage of this approach is that it may make it easier to link governance to popular debate within the public realm. Such linkages may increase the Bank's ability to pursue an effective policy dialogue which enhances the role of civil society in Africa as a buffer and a broker between government and society.

In short, democratisation and individual political rights are not prerequisites for an effective policy of governance. In both cases the institutions have the potential to make an impact on state–civil society relations. The question is whether in the future they have the ability and the willingness to walk the tightrope between consensus and controversy.

THE WAY AHEAD

Work and burden-sharing are important themes for the international development debate but so should role-sharing. Coined in the language of economics, the role of the AfDB and the ADB in the governance debate lies in their comparative advantage. As regional institutions, in which borrowing member countries have substantial influence, they are in a privileged situation to address the governance issue. However, in order to take on such a role the participants/actors in the Banks must keep in mind that, given their charters and the high degree of political sensitivity attached to individual political rights, democracy and democratisation should not perhaps form the main focus of these Banks' governance policies. On the contrary, these institutions should avoid these terms because they all too often send dialogue into a blind alley and place participants in rigid positions.

Building consensus is undoubtedly important but this should form just one element of the AfDB and the ADB work on governance. The other element which is required for an effective regional bank policy on governance is controversy. If individual political rights are not an integrated part of the governance/sound development management/institution building approach of the AfDB and the ADB, then at the very least their policies should have a broader focus than collective economic rights. If these Banks are going to have an edge in development policy and discourses in Africa and Asia they must have a particular focus on interaction within the public realm.

NOTES

1. The Commission's report was the outcome of an initiative of Willy Brandt which led to a meeting in Sweden and the presentation of a document entitled *Common Responsibility in the 1990s: The Stockholm Initiative on Global Security and Governance.*

2. The odd man out here is the European Bank of Reconstruction and Development (EBRD). Established in the wake of the collapse of communism, the thinking behind EBRD was that the shift in the structure of international politics offered liberalism an opportunity to link economic development with political liberalisation.
3. The Council is a permanent revolving body of eminent Africans whose function is to advise the Bank on critical aspects of development policy.
4. Unfortunately, due to declining concessional resources, any move to link country allocations to good governance is most likely to appear as one based on negative sanctions rather than positive sanctions.
5. The report was soon known as the Knox report after the chairman of the task force, David Knox, a former vice-president of the World Bank.
6. Letter from the Nordic-Indian-Swiss Executive Director Inga Björk-Klevby to the President of the AfDB Omar Kabbaj.
7. The names used on the various themes are the names used by the Bank. For some reason the Bank prefer in its official documents to talk about women-in-development instead of gender and gender issues.
8. For instance, in the OECD approach to governance democratic elections are held to be the general standard of accountability.
9. Equally important was the decision to distil the knowledge from the workshop into a book. The book – *Small Countries – Big Lessons: Governance and the rise of East Asia* written by Hilton Root [*1996*] is a serious attempt to formulate an Asian approach to governance. In short, his argument is that the uniqueness of East Asia lies in its capacity to implement successfully economic and social policies. Consequently, governance is defined as sound development management.
10. The first part of this section is strongly influenced by a World Bank document from 1991 entitled *Managing Development: The Governance Dimension*. This influence is acknowledged by the ADB in its policy paper on governance.

REFERENCES

ADB, 1982, *Agreement Establishing the Asian Development Bank*, Manila: ADB.
ADB, 1995a, *Governance*, Manila: ADB.
ADB, 1995b, *Governance: Sound Development Management*, Manila: ADB.
ADB, 1997, *News & Notes: Governance and Capacity Building at ADB*, Manila: ADB.
AfDB, 1964, *Agreement Establishing the African Development Bank*, Abidjan: AfDB.
AfDB, 1992, *Poverty Alleviation Strategy and Action Programme*, Abidjan: AfDB.
AfDB, 1994a, *The Democratisation Process in Africa, Governance and the Role of the African Development Bank: Recommendations of the AfDB African Advisory Council*, Abidjan: AfDB.
AfDB, 1994b, *Report of the Task Force on Project Quality*, Abidjan: AfDB.
AfDB, 1996a, *Inter-Office Memorandum: NIS Statement on the Sustainable Development Unit*, Abidjan: AfDB.
AfDB, 1996b, *Inter-Office Memorandum: Task Force on the Environment and Sustainable Development Unit (OESU)*, Abidjan: AfDB.
AfDB, 1996c, *Report on the Environment and Sustainable Development Unit*, Abidjan: AfDB.
Bøås, Morten, 1996, 'Environmental Policies and Multilateral Development Assistance: The Case of the African Development Bank and the Asian Development Bank', in Stein Hansen, Jan Hesselberg and Helge Hveem (eds.), *International Trade Regulation, National Development Strategies and the Environment: Towards Sustainable Development?*, Oslo: SUM, pp.195–226.
English, E. Philip and Harris M. Mule, 1996, *The African Development Bank*, Boulder, CO: Lynne Rienner Publishers.
Harbeson, John W., 1994, 'Civil Society and Political Renaissance in Africa', in John W. Harbeson, Donald Rothchild and Naomi Chazan (eds.), *Civil Society and the State in Africa*, Boulder, CO: Lynne Rienner Publishers, pp.1–29.
Hyden, Göran, 1992, 'Governance and the Study of Politics', in Göran Hyden and Michael Bratton (eds.), *Governance and Politics in Africa*, Boulder, CO: Lynne Rienner Publishers, pp.1–26.

Kappagoda, Nihal, 1995, *The Asian Development Bank*, Southampton: Intermediate Technology Publications.

OECD, 1995, *DAC Orientations on Participatory Development and Good Governance*, Paris: OECD.

Peprah, Ignatius, 1994, *The African Development Bank: Taking Stock and Preparing for the 21st Century*, Ottawa: C.-C. Consulting Ltd.

Report of the Commission on Global Governance, 1995, *Our Global Neighbourhood*, Oxford: Oxford University Press.

Root, Hilton, 1996, *Small Countries – Big Lessons: Governance and the Rise of East Asia*, Oxford: Oxford University Press.

Rosenau, James N., 1992, 'Governance and Change in World Politics', in James N. Rosenau and Ernst-Otto Czempiel (eds.), *Governance without Government: Order and Change in World Politics*, Cambridge: Cambridge University Press, pp.1–29.

World Bank, 1989, *Sub-Saharan Africa: From Crisis to Sustainable Growth*, Washington, DC: World Bank.

World Bank, 1991, *Managing Development: The Governance Dimension*, Washington, DC: World Bank

World Bank, 1992, *Governance and Development*, Washington, DC: World Bank.

Index

absolutism, 5ff, 14, 105
Africa 33f, 50, 51, 72, 73, 81, 91, 95, 115n, 18, 121, 132
African Charter on Human and People's Rights, 92
Development Bank (AIDB), 117–18, 120–24, 129ff, 133n
African Development Fund, 122
Albertyn, C., 80
American Declaration of Independence, 20
ANC, 73, 75, 79, 80
anthropology, 44–5, 47
apartheid, 70, 7 1 , 77
APREFA, 39, 48n
arab landholding (Kenya), 52, 55–7, 65, 66
Arnfred, S., 83
Asia, 72, 73, 1 18, 125, 127, 130, 131, 132
Asian Development Bank (ADB), I 17–18, 125–29, 130ff, 133n
Asian Development Fund, 127
Australia, 2
Ayatollah Khomeini, 21

Ba, B., 38
Bangladesh, 127
bantustan, 71 , 75, 79
Barthes, R., 9
Baxi, U., 3
Bernstein, H., 82
Bobbio, N., 3
bounded rationality, 37
Burkina Paso, 38, 40, 41, 48n

Canada, 2
capitalism, 35, 67, 105
Castoriadis, C., 1 I
Chagga, 35
Chavunduka, G.L., 93, 99
Chayanovian model, 75
China, 31, 127
Chitungwiza, 90, 93, 94
Christiansen, R., 74
chronopolitics, I l&12
civil society, 2, 1 19, 129–32
Cloete, M., 76, 82
Cold War, 39, 40
colonialism, 107, 109
Commission on Global Governance, 119, 127
Committee on Economic, Social and Cultural

Rights, 97
Committee on the Elimination of All Forms of Discrimination against Women (CEDAW), 92, 93, 97, 102n
Cornmunal Property Associations Act (1996) (South Africa), 75
communitarian values, 92
community court, 89, 99–100
community of rights, 26ff
community, cultural, 28
community, international, 40, 45, 130
community, political, I 9, 26, 28ff
community, the individual and, 109ff
conformity model, 108–9
Copernican revolution, 5
corruption, 33, 65, 79, 80, 1 19
Coulibaly, C., 42
Cranston, M., 91
Cross, C., 74, 76, 77, 78, 79, 82
customary law, 35, 43, 78, 83, 88ff, 107–8, 110, 113–14
Customary Marriages Act (Zimbabwe), 90

Dahl, T.S., 101
decentralisation, 37, 38, 40, 74, 125
democracy, 4, 26, 3 I , 33, 38, 40, 42, 75, 79, 105, 11 8, 121, 129ff
Department of Land Affairs (DLA), South Africa, 70, 74, 75, 77
Donnelly, 1., 96
DuToit, A., 82, 83
Dworkin, R., 24

Eales, K., 77, 79
East Africa, 34
Eastern Cape, 71 , 78
economic reductionism, 50–51
Elias, T.O., 43
England, 34
Europe, 31, 106, 107
Extension of Security of Tenure Act (1997) (South Africa), 75

Fabian, J., 11
family law, 89, 90, 102n, 106–7
Finland, 29
formal law, 105, 113, 114
Foucault, M., 15
France, 39

For Product Safety Concerns and Information please contact our EU
representative GPSR@taylorandfrancis.com
Taylor & Francis Verlag GmbH, Kaufingerstraße 24, 80331 München, Germany

www.ingramcontent.com/pod-product-compliance
Lightning Source LLC
Chambersburg PA
CBHW050532270326
41926CB00015B/3184